Pierre Bourdieu's Theory and Its Sociological Uses

Pierre Bourdieu's Theory and Its Sociological Uses

Under the Direction of
François de Singly

Anne Jourdain
Sidonie Naulin

Translated by
Siba Barkataki

AAKAR

PAP
TAGORE

The work is published with the support of the Publication Assistance Programmes of the Institutfrançais.

Originally published in France as:

La théorie de Pierre Bourdieu et ses usages sociologiques–Sociologies contemporaines, by Anne Jourdain and Sidonie Naulin

Armand Colin is a trademark of DUNOD Editeur–11, rue Paul Bert - 92240 MALAKOFF.

Pierre Bourdieu's Theory and Its Sociological Uses
Anne Jourdain and Sionie Naulin

English translation first published by Aakar Books, 2020

ISBN 978-93-5002-658-8

Published by
AAKAR BOOKS
28 E Pocket IV, Mayur Vihar Phase I
Delhi 110 091 India
www.aakarbooks.com

Laser Typeset at
Arpit Printographers, Delhi

Printed at
Sapra Brothers, Noida

Contents

Introduction 7

1. The Craft of Sociology **15**

1. SOCIOLOGY AS A SCIENCE

1.1 Resumption and Continuation of the Durkheimian Project 16

1.2 Is Sociology a Science Like the Others? (Jean–Clause Passeron, 1991) 21

2. SOCIOLOGY IN ACTION 26

2.1 The Methods of the Sociologist 26

2.2 Denaturalising the Social World: "Invention of the Third Age" (Rémi Lenoir, 1979) 34

3. A NEW CONCEPT OF ACTION 37

3.1. Genetic Structuralism 37

3.2 The Notion of Habitus 41

3.3 Habitus and Practical Reason: From Actor to Agent 44

2. Sociology of Education **49**

1. THE SCHOOL AS AN EXAMPLE OF SOCIAL REPRODUCTION 50

1.1 From Social Inequalities to Educational Inequalities 51

1.2 From Educational Inequalities to Social Inequalities 60

1.3 From Academic Controversy to Public Debate 67

2. THE QUESTION OF EDUCATIONAL DEMOCRATISATION (Stéphane Beaud, 2002) 71

3. Sociology of Culture **78**

1. THE THEORY OF CULTURAL LEGITIMACY 79

1.1 Homology Between Social Hierarchy and Cultural Hierarchy 80

1.2 Habitus as the Principle that Generates Cultural Practices 85

1.3 Taste, Between Imitation and Distinction 90

2. LEGITIMISATION OF A CULTURAL PRACTICE: EXAMPLE OF JAZZ (Jean-Louis Fabiani, 1986) 96

3. THE THEORY OF CULTURAL LEGITIMACY IN QUESTION 99
3.1 Eclecticism of Cultural Practices (Richard Peterson and Roger Kern, 1996) 99
3.2 Dissonant Cultural Practices and Preferences (Bernard Lahire, 2004) 101
3.3 Radical Critics of the Theory of Cultural Legitimacy 104

4. The Theory of Social Space 107
1. CAPITAL AND SOCIAL SPACE 107
1.1 Capital at the Foundation of a Multidimensional Social Space 107
1.2 The function of the concept of capital (François de Singly, 1987) 120
2. THE THEORY OF FIELDS 123
2.1 Field and Position within the Field 123
2.2 The Use of the Concept of Field: Example of the Literary Field (Pierre Bourdieu, 1992; Christophe Charle, 1977) 132
2.3 From the Economic Field to the Economy of Symbolic Goods 137

Conclusion 144

Bibliographic References 150

Introduction

Prominent sociologist of the twentieth century and committed intellectual till the end of his life, Pierre Bourdieu is the author of a general theory of social life. Drawing on the works of Karl Marx, Emile Durkheim and that of Max Weber, Pierre Bourdieu was interested in mechanisms of domination and reproduction of social hierarchies and in the link between social origins of individuals and their preferences and practices.

Pierre Bourdieu (1930-2002)

Pierre Bourdieu was born on August 1, 1930 in Denguin, in the Pyrénées-Atlantiques. He was the only child of a father belonging to the Bearnese small peasantry, who worked first as a farmhand, then a postman and went on to become the Postmaster of the village, and a mother who came from a family of landowners. Béarn, to which Pierre Bourdieu remained attached all his life, is the place where he conducted one of his first ethnographic surveys, and is also the subject of his last book, *Le Bal des célibataires. Crise de la société paysanne en Béarn*[1] (*The Bachelors' Ball: The Crisis of Peasant Society in Béarn*). Educated initially at the secondary school in Pau, Pierre Bourdieu then entered the *khâgne* or preparatory class for entrance exams at the Louis-le-Grand secondary school, in Paris. In 1951, he enrolled in the École normal supérieure de la rue d'Ulm and went on to obtain the *agrégation* or the highest teaching diploma in philosophy in 1954. He then started working on a doctoral thesis on philosophy, which remained unfinished, under the supervision of Georges Canguilhem. He worked simultaneously as a philosophy teacher, for a year, in the secondary school of Moulins.

His military obligations took him to Algeria from 1955 to 1960. This period was crucial for Pierre Bourdieu: it forged his passage from philosophy to sociology. In 1958, he published his first book, *Sociologie de l'Algérie*[2], (*The Sociology of Algeria*) in the "Que sais-je?" series. It was in Kabyle that Pierre Bourdieu carried out his first ethnographic research. These investigations led to several works, notably *Travail et travailleurs en Algérie*[3] (*Work and Workers in Algeria*) written in collaboration with Alain Darbel, Jean-Paul Rivet and Claude Seibel, and *Le Déracinement. La Crise de l'agriculture traditionnelles en Algérie*[4] (*The Uprooting: The Crisis of Traditional Agriculture in Algeria*) written with Abdelmalek Sayad. These books are sites of reflection on changes that took place in pre-capitalist societies (urbanisation, wage system, etc.) brought on by colonial capitalism and independence struggles. These texts are based on ethnographic researches as well as questionnaire-based surveys conducted with the help of Alain Darbel, a statistician in the *Institut national de la statistique et des études économiques*, INSEE (*French National Institute of Statistics and Economic Studies*) (INSEE). Later, Pierre Bourdieu's anthropological study of the Kabyle society serves as the empirical basis of his more theoretical books on human action such as *Esquisse d'une théorie de la pratique*[5] (*Outline of a theory of practice*) or *Sens Pratique*[6] (*The Logic of Practice*) and his writings dedicated to domination and gender relations.[7]

In 1960, Pierre Bourdieu returned to France. He started

working in the Sorbonne as assistant to the philosopher and sociologist Raymond Aron, founding general secretary of the *Centre de sociologie européenne*, CSE (*European Centre for Sociology*) established in 1960. Thereafter, Pierre Bourdieu was appointed as lecturer at the University of Lille, where he worked till 1964. That year he was appointed as Director of Studies at the École Pratique des Hautes Études (EPHE) and he also embarked upon editorial work while heading the publication of the book-series *Le Sens Commun* at the Éditions de Minuit. It is in this book-series that he published, till 1922, most of his books and those of his team members. He also edited works of classic French authors and translations of foreign authors that inspired him (Erving Goffman, Richard Hoggart, Erwin Panofsky). 1964 is also the year of publication of *Héritiers. Les étudiants et la culture*[8] (*The Inheritors. French Students and Their Relation to Culture*), co-authored with Jean-Claude Passeron. This, for Pierre Bourdieu, was the first book that had significant academic as well as commercial success. At that time, education and cultural practices were his subjects of predilection. He was also interested in the sociology of art. Along with other members of the CSE, he published in 1965 *Un Art moyen. Essai sur les usages sociaux de la photographie*[9] (*Photography, a Middlebrow Art*), thereafter in 1966 *L'Amour de l'Art. Les musées d'art européens et leur public*[10] (*The Love of Art: European Art Museums and Their Public*), which is a study on museum visitors. His interest in the sociology of art manifests itself again much later in Pierre Bourdieu's career, in 1922, when he writes *Les Règles de l'art. Genèse et structure du champ littéraire*[11] (*The Rules of Art: Genesis and Structure of the Literary Field*). In this book, he establishes a historical analysis of the constitution and functioning of the artistic "field" and in the process, proposes an iconic text on the sociological analysis of social fields.

In 1968, Pierre Bourdieu dissociated himself from his mentor Raymond Aron. He went ahead and founded the Centre for the Sociology of Education and Culture, currently known as the Centre de sociologie européenne (European Centre for Sociology) and that very same year he published with Jean-Claude Chamboredon and Jean-Claude Passeron *Le Métier de sociologue: préalables épistémologiques*[12] (*The Craft of Sociology. Epistemological Preliminaries*). In the events of May 1968, Pierre Bourdieu did not engage in public debate, although his book *Les Héritiers (The Inheritors*) was cited extensively. Two years later, in 1970, Pierre Bourdieu co-authored with Jean-Claude Passeron *La Reproduction. Éléments pour une théorie du système d'enseignement*[13] (*Reproduction in Education, Society and Culture*) a new text on education that was more theoretical than *Les Héritiers*. The authors demonstrate that the schooling system, far from offering a genuine platform of equal opportunities, actually contributes to the legitimisation of the social hierarchy.

During the 1970s, Pierre Bourdieu began to play an increasingly pivotal role in the sociological landscape. His influence exceeded that of sociologists who were his contemporaries (Michel Crozier, Georges Friedmann and Alain Touraine) with whom incidentally he barely communicated. Pierre Bourdieu's dominant position was, in part, established by the community that he brought together around him. A rare phenomenon in the field of social sciences, Bourdieu surrounded himself with a team of sociologists who contributed to his work (book reviews, conducting surveys, etc.) and who participated in the dissemination of his thoughts. In 1975, Pierre Bourdieu launched the review *Actes de la Recherche en Sciences Sociales* that he directed till his death. The review allowed him to expound his works and those of his colleagues and students. Its form was relatively new (illustrations, large format, innovative page layout), but the functioning of the review was often denounced as autocratic. In 1979, Pierre Bourdieu published his major work *La Distinction. Critique sociale du jugement*[14] (*Distinction: A Social Critique of the Judgement of Taste*). Notions such as "habitus" and "capital" that are central to the Bourdieusian theory were widely mobilised in order to communicate the differences in cultural practices based on social classes.

In the early 1980s, the key concepts of Bourdieusian sociology were already established. In the twenty years that followed, Pierre Bourdieu, while continuing to pursue his prolific work, focused increasingly on the dissemination of his theories, especially internationally. At the same time, he was being increasingly recognised by French institutions. In 1981, he was elected Professor at the Collège de France and in 1993 he was the first sociologist to be awarded the CNRS Gold Medal.

The last ten years of Pierre Bourdieu's life were marked by his transition from the role of a university researcher to that of a committed intellectual. In 1993, he was director of the edited volume *La Misère du monde*[15] (*The Weight of the World*) which, through life stories of individuals in situations of social suffering, established Pierre Bourdieu as the voice of people in spaces of social destitution. This edited collection was a massive bestseller. At the same time, there was an increase in Pierre Bourdieu's activist engagement in the 1990s. He especially came to the defence of strikers during the social movement, in the autumn of 1995, he then endorsed the winter protest of the unemployed in 1997-98 and the alter-globalists. His criticism of neoliberalism and of policies that advocate the dismantling of public services were widely communicated by the media with which he had an otherwise turbulent relationship marked by fascination and radical criticism. Two texts, entitled *Contre-*

feux 1[16] and 2[17] (*Firing Back: Against the Tyranny of the Market*) bring together his political interventions. To further support his activist engagement, Pierre Bourdieu started a new editorial collaboration with the Editions du Seuil in 1992 and in the wake of the workers' strikes of 1995, he launched, the publishing house "Raison d'agir" in association with Le Seuil. It is with Raison d'agir that he published the slim controversial book *Sur la Télévision*[18] (*On Television*) in 1996. The book was easily accessible to a wider public and it soon became his bestselling book. In 2000, Pierre Carles in his documentary film *La sociologie est un sport de combat*[19] (*Sociology is a Martial Art*) traces Pierre Bourdieu's intellectual and political commitment. He especially highlights the influence that the sociologist had on social movements. Alongside his activist engagement, Pierre Bourdieu pursued a more academic reflection on sociology and the role of science: *Méditations Pascaliennes*[20] (*Pascalian Meditations*); *Science de la science et réflexivité*[21] (*Science of Science and Reflexivity*)...

Pierre Bourdieu died on January 23, 2002, at the age of 71, leaving behind him a monumental body of work (343 publications according to the French daily *Libération* (January 1, 2002). His biggest editorial successes were his polemical books for the general public (*Sur la télévision, La Misère du monde*). His more theoretical books such as *Les Héritiers* or *La Distinction,* are considered to be classic texts of sociology.

Presentation of the Book

The objective of this book, dedicated to Pierre Bourdieu's theory and its sociological uses, is to reconstitute concisely and accurately the principal contributions of this author to the field of sociology. This in particular, includes facilitating the reading of Pierre Bourdieu's texts, known for their complex writing, comprising of stylistic contortions and word play.

Although Pierre Bourdieu's sociological works have covered a wide range of subjects throughout his career (traditional society, academic world, media, economy, etc.), we will focus here on the four central themes that form the core of his work. The first chapter is based on Bourdieu's epistemological thought process which he developed throughout his life. Understanding his idea of sociology and the work of a sociologist gives a point of entry to understand how Pierre Bourdieu views the social world and the world of human action. The two chapters that follow take two key objects of Bourdieusian reflection as starting points, education and culture, in order to highlight the empirical process that shaped the author's fundamental concepts. The idea is to demonstrate, in both cases, how these concepts have enabled a more profound and permanent renewal of deliberations carried out in these domains. Finally, the last chapter talks about the theory of social space. This theory explains the functioning of different domains of social life from a much broader and general perspective.

In each chapter, the demonstration of Pierre Bourdieu's theory is further articulated by the presentation of the author's works that illustrate and develop his arguments. This book aims to re-evaluate the scope of Pierre Bourdieu's sociological work, that is an indispensable reference point for many fields of study.

1

The Craft of Sociology

Pierre Bourdieu owes his fame to his theory of the social world. However, not entirely content with his practice of sociology, Bourdieu dedicated a part of his work to the reflection of conditions that determine the existence of sociology as a discipline, and to what was expected of a sociologist. These concerns arose as a result of the collective work done with two other sociologists: Jean-Claude Chamboredon and Jean-Claude Passeron. In 1968, the three sociologists published *Le Métier de sociologue*.[22] This book spells out the principles that should be followed in any sociological process in order to qualify as a scientific method. Revisiting the ways in which Pierre Bourdieu views the scientific nature of sociology followed by his views on human action helps to shed light on his theory of the social world.

1. SOCIOLOGY AS A SCIENCE

Any discipline that aims to be recognised as a science must examine the conditions of scientificity in its production of knowledge. This perspective, defined as "epistemological" has been applied to sociology since its very conception towards the end of the nineteenth century, notably in the works of Emile Durkheim (1858-1917). Pierre Bourdieu, along with Jean-Claude Chamboredon and Jean-Claude Passeron, raise this very issue in *Le Métier de sociologue*.

1.1 Resumption and Continuation of the Durkheimian Project

Intellectual Affiliation

The need to reflect on the conditions that sociology as a field needed to fulfil in order to be considered as a scientific discipline was initiated in France by Emile Durkheim at the end of the nineteenth century. At that time, sociology still in its infancy needed, in order to establish itself as an autonomous discipline, to highlight what distinguished it from other closely related disciplines such as psychology, philosophy, history and biology. Sociologists were also expected to reflect on processes that were capable of generating scientific knowledge. The solution proposed by Emile Durkheim in *Les Règles de la méthode sociologique*[23] (*The Rules of Sociological Method*) clearly states that it is possible to have a scientific understanding of the social world but, that, it bases itself less on the distinctiveness of its object of study (social life is also studied by historians as well as in the field of psychology) than on the methods that it uses.

More than seventy years later, Pierre Bourdieu, Jean-Claude Chamboredon and Jean-Claude Passeron, reinstated Emile Durkheim, somewhat forgotten in the meantime, as their principal point of reference while writing *Le Métier de sociologue.* Just like Durkheim, these three sociologists wished to come to a consensus with fellow sociologists of their time on factors that made sociology a scientific discipline and to discern the principles that should guide the work of a sociologist.

What mainly concerned the three authors was not so much the discussion on the pertinence of sociology's ranking amongst other scientific disciplines since the fact that sociology was a science seemed to have been already established (Pierre Bourdieu wrote: "Sociology seems to me to have all the properties that define a science"[24]), but rather "to question sociological practices", that is, to reflect on the social conditions in which techniques used by sociologists to take cognisance of the real, led to results that qualified as scientific: "The question of whether sociology is or is not a science, and a science like others, should be replaced by the question on the type of organisation and functioning of the scientific city most conducive to the appearance and development of research that is subject to strictly scientific controls" (*Le Métier de sociologue*, 1968, p. 103).

By raising this issue, the authors wanted, in particular, to denounce the absence of reflection on the use of statistical methods that were widely used towards the end of the 1960s under the guidance of the American sociologist Paul Lazarsfeld. For Pierre Bourdieu, Jean-Claude Chamboredon and Jean-Claude Passeron, this meant establishing a new theory of sociological practice.

With this aim in mind, they initially intended to write a three-volume work: the first volume would lay down the epistemological preliminaries of sociological knowledge (i.e. to define the conditions under which sociology is a science), the second book would analyse how a sociologist "constructs" his object of study (in other words, how he defines his problem question) and the third would draw up a critical repertoire of tools used in sociology.

Of the three books, only the first book *Le Métier de sociologue* as we know it today, was actually written. A special feature of this book is that the first half of the book has been written by the three authors while the other half is composed of illustrative texts drawn as much from sociology (Émile Durkheim, Max Weber, Marcel Mauss) as from the epistemological tradition originating from reflections on natural sciences (Gaston Bachelard, Georges Canguilhem, Alexandre Koyré).

Breaking Away from the Illusion of Immediate Knowledge

One of the most important lessons of Emile Durkheim in *Les Règles de la méthode sociologique* is that in order to observe and scientifically report social phenomena, sociologists need to "systematically take distance from prenotions". Prenotions are "schematic and summary representations" that are "formed by and for experience" by individuals and as a result, by sociologists as well. In fact, from the moment we start living in societies, we form useful representations for orientation, that help us to adopt a point of view and form our opinions...on the world around us. Just as, for instance, we have a perception of social hierarchies or of judicial activities in our country, but have no way of telling if these interpretations truly reflect reality, since our perceptions are not subjected to analysis. Such *a priori* ideas are obstacles to science as they prevent us from seeing the real nature of things.

Taking their cue from Emile Durkheim, the authors of *Métier de sociologue* warn against the danger of this "illusion of immediate knowledge" and encourage sociologists to bring about an "epistemological break" with this form of "spontaneous sociology" so as to be able to articulate a scientific discourse on the social world.

To steer clear of prenotions, Emile Durkheim advised sociologists to adopt a position that was external to social facts (social facts needed to be observed like things that were external to sociologists) and a prior position of ignorance. Various methods and techniques enabling this epistemological break have been elaborated in his works. *Le Métier de sociologue* talks about one such technique that involved assigning a temporary definition to the object of study. This definition is not based on personal impressions but rather on empirical signs that can be objectively observed in the object. In doing so, prenotions are partly neutralised, thus preventing the results of the investigation from being predetermined. Emile Durkheim, for instance, defined a crime as any punishable act. This allowed him to dissociate his research from his personal, moral judgements; judgements influenced by his skewed perception formed by incomplete knowledge of crime. Besides assigning provisional definitions to their objects, sociologists can also use techniques of objectification of the real world such as statistics. This is what Emile Durkheim used in *Le Suicide*[25] (*Suicide*). Based on statistical data on suicides in France, he highlighted patterns (seasonality of suicides, change in the rate of suicide depending on age) which led him to conclude that it was possible to explain suicides without referring to individuals' psychological motivations like prenotions would have us believe. The statistical tool by revealing unexpected results renders the social fact more objective, thus enabling us to go beyond our subjective prenotions.

The struggle against the illusion of immediate knowledge is however hindered by the nature of language used by sociologists. Pierre Bourdieu, Jean-Claude Chamboredon and Jean-Claude Passeron have stressed that one of the roadblocks to an epistemological break between common wisdom and the scientific discourse is caused by the fact that sociologists express themselves in the same language as the layperson. This does not hold true, for example, for physicists, who, thanks to the mathematical language and scientific vocabulary that is specific to their discipline, are able to easily distance their object of study from their personal interpretation. The common language used by sociologists is potentially a source of error because it contains perceptions of the social world. As stated by the authors: "Ordinary language [..] carries in its vocabulary and syntax a petrified philosophy of the social, always ready to spring out of the common words, or complex expressions made out of common words, that the sociologist inevitably uses" (pp. 36-37). Talking about the social ladder for instance, implicitly assumes that society is a fluid space within which it is possible to circulate between social scales, which is not the case when we talk of social classes. Sociologists should therefore continuously subject their language to critical analysis and distil their notions so as to separate any implicit presuppositions. Otherwise, they run the risk of mistaking objects reconstituted within and by common language as data.

Sociology of Disclosure

The distrust of individual discourse is another point that connects the authors of *Métier de sociologue* to Émile Durkheim. This suspicion stems from the principle that believes in "explaining the social through the social" (*Les Règles de la méthode sociologique*). In fact, to separate sociology from psychology, Emile Durkheim endeavoured to show that social facts (such as suicide) could be explained using other social facts (strength of community life, absence of norms) without resorting to biological (special suicidal physiology) or psychological explanations (emotional state...). This goes in tandem with a holistic view of social life according to which society as a whole goes beyond individuals, constraints and institutions that form it. This vision goes against the individualist concept of the social world wherein it is possible to analyse society by only studying its individuals. Pierre Bourdieu toes the same intellectual line as Emile Durkheim. Right from the moment when individuals are considered to be in part determined by the society that surpasses them, it follows that they are no longer aware of factors that determine what they do and who they are: this is the "principle of non-consciousness". While individuals might think that their actions are nothing but a result of their will, it is possible for the sociologist to objectify the factors that determine them, but in order to do so, he has to distance himself from the discourse of social actors.

Thus Pierre Bourdieu's sociology intends to be a sociology of disclosure that brings to light the determinisms that weigh upon social actors without them knowing it. In fact, social mechanisms are not immediately visible and the work of a sociologist is to make them appear. It is only when they are conscious of that which compels them, can they free themselves: "If the sociologist has a role, it is probably more to furnish weapons than to give lessons" (*Questions de sociologie*, 1984, p. 95).

The epistemological framework elaborated in *Le Métier de sociologue* provides a foundation from which to carry out a renewed study of the field of sociology. Amongst the authors who continued the work started by Pierre Bourdieu and his colleagues was Jean-Claude Passeron.

1.2 Is Sociology a Science Like the Others?
(Jean-Clause Passeron, 1991)

Jean-Claude Passeron co-authored *Le Métier de sociologue* in 1968 with Pierre Bourdieu and Jean-Claude Chamboredon. He further continued his epistemological research in *Le Raisonnement sociologique* (*Sociological Reasoning*) published in 1991.[26] His reflection started much before his work in *Le Métier de sociologue* which he began with the definitive premise that sociology was a science. Jean-Claude Passeron, on the contrary, questioned the scientificity of sociology: is sociology a science like the others?

The Point in Question

Le Raisonnement Sociologique sets out with two questions on sociology: "Science or not? If yes, like the others or not?" (p. 7). In this book, it is the comparison between the scientificity of sociology and that of the other experimental sciences (the natural sciences), that forms the basis of the methodological guidelines developed by Jean-Claude Passeron.

According to Jean-Claude Passeron, sociology is not different from the other human and social sciences (history, anthropology) which he categorises under the generic term "historical sciences". All these fields have one common object: the historical world. The latter is different from the object studied in experimental sciences insofar as the historical world is the space where phenomena is always contextualised and can never be reproduced identically. The scientists are thus denied the possibility to conduct experiments in the same way as other scientists as they can never control the conditions in which events occur. The criterion of scientificity inherent in experimental sciences cannot be applied to historical sciences. Yet, should historical sciences be excluded from the scientific universe? In other words, is there only a single unique system of scientificity?

Obstacles to the Constitution of Sociology as a Science

The fact that in sociology the object of study is the historical world where the same configurations can never be reproduced identically not only complicates the process of conducting experiments, but also prevents the process of establishing general laws. The theories proposed by the social sciences are in reality indexed to a specific spatio-temporal context, which prevents them from functioning like scientific paradigms. A paradigm is a theory on which scientists come to a consensus at a given moment, till the same is refuted by a new paradigm (thus in physics, Einstein's relativity paradigm replaced that of Newton). On the other hand, in historical sciences, different theories can coexist at a given moment.

Moreover, as already demonstrated by the authors of *Métier de sociologue*, sociologists express in the same language as laypersons, i.e. in "natural" or ordinary language, as opposed to an artificial or "protocol" language such as mathematics. For scientists to agree on a paradigm, they must have a common language, that is unequivocal and "stabilised", which means that it is founded on a "high degree of consensus" (p. 362) of a group of specialists. Consequently, "the weakness of any sociological discourse" (p. 371) stems from its inability to establish a protocol-based language that would contain [..] the virtues of a sustainable paradigm"(p. 371).

The concepts thus elaborated oscillate between two models: either they are extremely specific (which means that they specifically portray the contextual anchor of the phenomenon described) but their empirical precision prevents one from placing the discourse in a broader context, or they are "excessively" theoretical and cover a large number of situations, but are however incapable of accurately reporting a situation since they are indexed to a specific spatial or temporal context. This however does not imply that sociologists should renounce the process of conceptualisation. They have to take cognisance of the fact that their concepts are more likely to be, at best "incomplete abstractions", in other words, concepts that maintain a tacit reference to contextualisation. Jean-Claude Passeron thus concludes—while opposing the plan to produce the third volume of *Métier de Sociologue*—that "the scientific lexicon of sociology is an infeasible lexicon" (p. 371).

Conditions of Production of Scientific Sociological Knowledge

Jean-Claude Passeron highlights two techniques that could enable the use of sociology in a scientific manner while taking into account, at the same time, the distinctive characteristics resulting from the historical dimension of the discipline. These two methods resonate, to a great extent, the recommendations that Pierre Bourdieu, Jean-Claude Chamboredon and Passeron himself had made back in 1968 in *Métier de Sociologue,* but they are based on a slightly different premise.

The first technique involves the "protocolarisation" of natural language with the help of comparative reasoning. Despite the irreducibly historical nature of the social world, sociologists can agree to consider certain un-identical contexts as equivalents, by reassembling them together under the same category, in order to give a broader reach to their concepts. Similarly in *Métier de Sociologue,* Jean-Claude Passeron directs attention to the comparative reasoning that is built on ideal types or analogies. This form of reasoning, that enables either the comparison or the distinction between different historical contexts, can only lead to general conclusions, having a status similar to "presumptions". For conclusions to be considered as "necessity", there has to be an experimental reasoning where all the parameters are controlled, which is impossible when it comes to observing the historical world.

The second technique involves moving back and forth between experimental reasoning and historical contextualisation. Despite having a historical object of study, historical sciences can resort to experimental methods, such as using statistics. Before going any further, Jean-Claude Passeron reiterates his call for an epistemological vigilance to sociologists from the moment they start using experimental methods. He makes this appeal especially because sociologists, as a result of expressing in a formalised language, tend to fall prey to "experimentalist illusions" (i.e. the belief according to which the recourse to experimental methods is a sufficient guarantee of the scientificity of the results). Nonetheless, Jean-Claude Passeron insists, more than he did in *Métier de Sociologue*, on the complementarity between experimental reasoning and the historical narrative. Both these methods are intrinsically in opposition: while the first method is based on the observation, under monitored parameters, of consistent correlations between social facts, which results in the phenomenon being deindexed from its particular historical context, the second method, on the other hand, accurately indexes the interpretation of historical facts to their spatial and temporal contexts. The problem which arises is that a sociology that is a simple historical narrative risks being reduced to spontaneous sociology or history and a sociology that is based on statistics will be devoid of any historical meaning. Experimental reasoning in sociology is thus inseparable from the work of historical contextualisation: "Sociological reasoning distinguishes itself from the historical narrative through *moments of experimental reasoning*, however [..] these purist methodological moments inevitably alternate with other moments of natural reasoning during interpretative analysis. [..] Statistical reasoning [..] remains very much a form of experimental reasoning only as long as it refrains from deliberating on the historical world: as soon as some meaning is introduced while communicating its formal correlations, the statements acquire a context, spoken or implied." (p. 78)

The conclusion reached in *Le Raisonnement sociologique* is that sociology is very much a science, but its scientificity should not be measured in light of the criteria applied to natural sciences. Therefore there exists different domains of scientificity and "natural reasoning is not reduced to common wisdom" (p. 12). Thus, while aligning with some of the conclusions of *Métier de sociologue,* Jean-Claude Passeron gives further nuances to the Bourdieusian affirmation by stating that "sociology [...] seems to have all the characteristics that define a science."[27]

2. SOCIOLOGY IN ACTION

Besides an epistemological reflection on the conditions that need to be fulfilled by sociology to qualify as a science, Pierre Bourdieu, Jean-Claude Chamboredon and Jean-Claude Passeron put forward in *Le Métier de Sociologue* in 1968 an analysis of the methods used by sociologists. In the book, the authors agree that the methods that lead to an "epistemological rupture" must be controlled in order to ensure the scientificity of the results generated. Whether it means employing statistics, observation or interviews, the sociologist should maintain an "epistemological vigilance" during the construction of his object of research and during data collection.

2.1 The Methods of the Sociologist

Although *Le Métier de Sociologue* broaches the question of the methods used by sociologists, the approach remains essentially theoretical and abstract. Also, it is futile to look for "recipes", "tips" or "secrets" in this book that can be used by the amateur sociologist starting a field investigation. The authors' interest for methodology is articulated in their questioning of the specific nature of the sociological process, conceived as a scientific process.

The Importance of Epistemological Control of Methods

"Fact is conquered, constructed and tested": this statement by Gaston Bachelard has been quoted by Pierre Bourdieu,

Jean-Claude Chamboredon and Jean-Claude Passeron when presenting the three "epistemological acts" that form, according to them, the foundation of sociology. These three "acts" do not represent three distinct moments of research, but they can be found in every stage of a sociological investigation. First, the fact needs to be "conquered" from the illusion of immediate knowledge: as we have seen before, a break has to be made with respect to common language in order to introduce sociology within the domain of scientificity. The fact is also "constructed" according to the theoretical proposition to which the chosen methodology is aligned. It is in accordance to this theoretical questioning and the corresponding methodology that the fact is "tested", that is, put into practice. If these three epistemological tests do not succeed one another during the research, they nevertheless follow a hierarchy: the test (or experimentation) depends on the construction, which in turn, depends on the break. Since the notion of the break has already been introduced, we will focus further on the process of construction and that of testing as well as on the link established between these two epistemological acts.

In sociology "pure" data that can be detached from theory does not exist. The assessment always depends on the construction of the object that in itself is inevitably theoretical: a theoretical framework is vital for the interrogation of reality. For example, to carry out an observation, the sociologist must draw on theoretical postulations that give direction to his research: he must know what he needs to observe in order to establish his analysis. Any observation table, that draws up a list of aspects that a sociologist must pay attention to, thus puts theoretical premises into action. Likewise, the questionnaire of a statistical survey is based on hypotheses that tend to shape the results: the answers obtained depend on the questions asked. Insofar as the questionnaire determines the results that one can obtain, the construction of the object appears to be a fundamental scientific act: "the facts that validate the theory are only as good as the theory they validate" (p. 85).

If, contrary to popular belief, research techniques are not neutral but are instead steeped in theory, the sociologist has to be vigilant when using them. Pierre Bourdieu, Jean-Claude Chamboredon and Jean-Claude Passeron talk of an "epistemological vigilance".

Finally, the sociologist has to break away from two types of illusions: the illusion of immediate knowledge, which must be opposed to the principle of rupture owing mainly to the recourse made to sociological methods, and the scientistic illusion of the neutrality of research techniques, which must be opposed to the rigorous epistemological monitoring of methods used.

Breaking Away from the Statistical Illusion

Having recourse to statistics allows to break away from immediate knowledge. We will see in the following chapters that a number of sociological results declared by Pierre Bourdieu are derived from statistical analysis. Nevertheless, the authors of *Métier de Sociologue* warn us about the use of statistics which detaches itself from any reflection on the theoretical implications of the method. In particular, the development of the questionnaire that collects data cannot take place without questioning the assumptions that are inherent in the questions. Each of the questions points to an implicit theoretical concern that the sociologist must be aware of if he wishes to accurately interpret the answers collected during his survey. Otherwise, the sociologist runs the risk of reifying his own theoretical suppositions by inappropriately interpreting his questions as questions that his subjects essentially ask themselves. In the absence of any epistemological control, his method cannot thus be deemed scientific.

In a text entitled "L'opinion publique n'existe pas"[28] ("Public Opinion Doesn't Exist"), Pierre Bourdieu shows that opinion polls depend on unexamined assumptions and that their results can consequently be challenged. By countering each one of the three fundamental assumptions, he deconstructs the notion of public opinion as outlined by polling organisations. The first assumption states that: "everybody can have an opinion ; in other words, [..] the production of opinion is within everyone's reach" (p. 222). Pierre Bourdieu demonstrates, on the contrary, that political skill is unequally distributed in accordance with the level of education. The exclusion of non-responses in the presentation of results allows to resolve the problem of the respondents' differential abilities to form an opinion, especially political. Furthermore, the questions are interpreted differently by the respondents, depending on their social background and their respective value systems. These arguments tend to discredit the assumption put forward by polling organisations who claim that the conditions of opinion production are consistently and universally fulfilled. According to the second assumption, "all opinions matter" (p. 222) and simply adding them will form what we call a "public opinion". "Public opinion" thus constituted, corresponds to what Pierre Bourdieu calls an "*artefact*", that is, a construct moulded by a research technique which does not have an equivalent in reality. He further adds that it is an artefact that is deprived of any meaning since public opinion cannot be summarised by a percentage figure. In reality, a public opinion is an outcome of opinion leaders and pressure groups who manage to successfully mobilise themselves and make their demands heard in the political arena. Individual opinions do not all have the same weight in the constitution of a public opinion. Finally, Pierre Bourdieu confronts the "hypothesis which states that there is a consensus on the problems, in other words, there is an agreement on the questions that are worth asking" (p. 222). While calling into question the autonomy of the polling organisations, he shows that the questions asked during an opinion poll are directly linked to the preoccupations of the political staff who want to be informed about the ways in which they can organise their work. As a result of this "problem imposition", the questions asked are not the real questions that are actually posed by the people interrogated. Ultimately, "public opinion" which is constructed by polling organisations do not exist in reality: it is only a pure artefact that depends on implicit assumptions.

Pierre Bourdieu's text is instructive at two levels. Firstly, he reiterates caution against statistical illusion that may arise due to the less than rigorous usage of quantitative methods, both by the sociologist and by the statistician of the polling organisation. Secondly, the text appears to be an application of the principle of break defended in the *Le Métier de Sociologue:* the notion of public opinion has been deconstructed by revealing the assumptions on which it is based. The polemical title—"Public opinion does not exist"—insists that the expressions that stem from common language should not be taken for granted.

Breaking Away from the Biographical Illusion

Pierre Bourdieu's enquiry into the way in which methods of research influence the results obtained, also focuses on the biographical interview. His text "L'illusion biographique"[29] ("Biographical Illusion"), is a reference point with respect to methodological reflection on "life history". Theoretical assumptions that underlie this particular method are analysed in his text: "To talk of life history, is to presume in the least, and that is not insignificant, that life is a story and that a life is an inextricable ensemble of events of an individual existence that is conceived as a story and the narrative of this story" (p. 81). Within the framework of a biographical interview, it is in the interests of both the interviewer and the interviewee to accept the *"postulate of the meaning of narrated existence"* (p. 82). Thus, in the course of the interview, the interviewee—prompted by the interviewer—tends to give meaning to the disparate events that he recounts. He becomes the "ideologist of his own life" (p. 82) and his narrative is nothing but a retrospective reconstruction that aims to establish the coherence of his narrative flow. "Since I was very young", "I have always been", "even at that time", etc., are expressions very often found in interviews: through these rhetorical procedures, the interviewee justifies the reasons of his commitment by offering a coherence to his entire progression.

The biographical interview does not permit to make a break with common sense. In fact, it is inseparable from the ordinary language that describes life like a career, a chalked out journey, a linear movement. The technique of enquiry corresponding to the story of life appears therefore to be inevitably imprinted with biographical illusion. While statistical analysis, if uncontrolled, runs the risk of leading the sociologist to a scientistic illusion, biographical illusion limits itself to the illusion of immediate knowledge described in *Le Métier de Sociologue*. In "Biographical Illusion", Pierre Bourdieu seems to finally prohibit the use of the biographical interview as a technique of research allowing to break with common sense which gives access to a scientific mode of explanation of the social world.

In reality, Pierre Bourdieu himself resorts to the biographical interview method. In 1993, he published *La Misère du monde*[30] (*The Weight of the World*) that recreates life narratives of workers, employees and farmers giving an account of their suffering and misery[31]. More than a hundred and fifty interviews were thus conducted between 1989 and 1992 by a research team of twenty-two sociologists directed by Pierre Bourdieu. The publication of the book is often considered as a break with respect to the epistemological reflections developed, especially in *Le Métier de sociologue* or in "L'illusion biographique". Pierre Bourdieu seems to finally grant to the biographical interview, that is to the subjective narrative of individuals' lives, the right to figure among other valid sociological methods of research. He however never explains as to how a sociologist can break away from biographical illusion. On the other hand, he looks at ways in which the sociologist can exercise a rigorous epistemological control of interview situations. By shifting the problem, he attaches his questions to a certain number of preoccupations articulated in *Métier de sociologue.* Therefore, in the text "Comprendre" ("Understanding") placed at the end of *La Misère du monde,* he insists on the importance of controlling the effects of the interview in order to fight "against the illusion that consists in looking for neutrality in the dissolution of the observer" (p. 916). The scene of the interview has to be analysed in order to abandon the illusion of its neutrality and understand the ways in which it can influence the remarks collected. If the sociologist has to look at ways to reduce the distortions arising from the social asymmetry between the interviewer and the interviewee and thus try to alleviate the "symbolic violence" (see Chapter 2) in the relation, he can do it only through a profound reflection on what can be said and what cannot. The comprehensive perspective (adopted by the sociologist Max Weber) newly demonstrated by Pierre Bourdieu, that involves looking into subjective reasoning and therefore into the meaning that individuals assign to their actions (contrary to the explanatory perspective), relies on a continuous work of construction aiming at obtaining answers that are least influenced by the effects of interview situations.

Self-Analysis at the Heart of Epistemological Vigilance

In *Le Métier de Sociologue,* Pierre Bourdieu, Jean-Claude Chamboredon and Jean-Claude Passeron clarify that epistemological vigilance not only concerns assumptions specific to the techniques of survey but also deals with the social conditions surrounding the sociological practice that need to be objectified. The sociologist is not actually a disembodied being: he is a social subject characterised by his social allegiance, gender, age, likes and dislikes. As a result, he unconsciously forms a certain number of preconceptions with respect to his object of research. Thus, assumptions regarding a professional practice (like that of an advocate), sporting activities (golf, for instance) or certain family situations (such as divorce) would vary depending on whether the researcher belongs to the working class or comes from the upper middle class. Consequently, in order to bring these assumptions to light and to detect their influence on the results obtained, the sociologist is duty-bound to analyse his own relation to the object studied. This reflexivity, at the centre of the sociological process, allows a greater control over formulated conclusions. According to the three authors, it is a question of escaping the ethnocentrism that corresponds to the "assumption about the absence of assumptions" (p. 100). The sociologist is thus prompted to do a self-analysis, which involves considering himself as a sociological object, and doing a sociology of himself and that of his relation to sociology. In order to comply with this principle, Pierre Bourdieu, towards the end of his life, wrote *Esquisse pour une auto-analyse*[32] (*Sketch for a Self-Analysis*). This book should not be read like an autobiography, but as a way for Pierre Bourdieu to bring to light his assumptions about sociology, linked to his particular social grounding. This book was widely criticised. It was particularly reproached for not having attained its objective, as the sociologist remained silent about certain structural aspects of his trajectory, his social origin and his family life among other other things.

2.2 Denaturalising the Social World: "Invention of the Third Age" (Rémi Lenoir, 1979)

The principle of rupture defended in *Le Métier de sociologue* can be illustrated through the works of Rémi Lenoir on the invention of the third age. Rémi Lenoir is a Bourdieusian sociologist who completed his thesis under the supervision of Pierre Bourdieu. He is a member of the research team in the CSE (Centre de sociologie européenne), and he especially contributed to writing *La Misère du monde* (1993). In 1979, he published an article entitled "L'invention du troisième âge. Constitution du champ des agents de gestion de la vieillesse"[33] ("Invention of the Third Age. Constitution of a Field of Agents for the Management of Old Age") in the *Actes de la Recherche en Sciences Sociales*, a journal edited by Pierre Bourdieu. He focuses on the historical genesis of the "third age" category. Having first established that the "third age" is linked to the generalisation of pension schemes and to the transformation of inter-generational relationships, he further defends the theory which posits that the maintenance and development of this category is supported by the emergence of institutions and specialists who take an interest in their existence and contribute to redefining old age as a "new lease of life" or as a "time for leisure".

The Historical Genesis of the "Third Age" Category

According to Rémi Lenoir, the "subject of pensions" emerged towards the middle of the nineteenth century, with the ageing of the first generation of workers. By the end of the nineteenth century, there were worker struggles in favour of pensions since the elderly became a burden for the working class families. Following the 1928-1930 social insurance legislation, mandatory pension systems were implemented and in 1945, at the time of the creation of social security, these systems were extended to all categories of employees: the pensioners thus formed an autonomous age group. It is finally in the 1960s that the notion of the "third age" appears, with the increase in the number of elderly people and pensioners. In 1962, the Laroque Report, in particular, offers a new concept of old age by highlighting a "policy for the elderly" which not only applies to the most deprived old people but to the entire elderly population. The problem of the elderly is thus permanently detached from that of destitution. The Laroque Commission encouraged the constitution of a field of management of the elderly, thus unifying actions and discourses which were till then isolated.

The rise of the supplementary pension system, as well as the emergence of assisted living facilities and specialised clubs, and even the development of gerontology as the science of ageing, all form part of the new representation of old age which reinforces the notion of the "third age". Institutions and agents who specialise in the management of old age contribute to imposing this representation. By associating the "third age" to a "new lease of life", they legitimise the creation of their profession. By instilling the idea that life "begins at sixty", they help to establish a new market where the key participants are the middle class elderly who struggle because of the disruption caused by retirement. The third age clubs or workshops enable them, for instance, to transform idle time into leisure time or even into opportunities to cultivate themselves. Rémi Lenoir concludes that: "The symbolic manipulation of the social image of old age does not only have symbolic effects" but it "contributes, [on the contrary] by naming them, in establishing and imposing new needs, especially the need for specialists responsible for ensuring the satisfaction of those needs" (p. 78).

Breaking with the Principle of Denaturalisation

Rémi Lenoir's article offers a practical understanding of the principle of rupture defended in *Le Métier de sociologue*. Initially, the "third age" appears to be a category arising from ordinary language, which is accompanied by a set of prenotions. The work of the sociologist lies in breaking with this common meaning and studying, especially with the help of archives, the history behind the emergence of this category. By showing that the "third age" did not always exist, the sociologist denaturalises the notion.

The denaturalisation of the social world is a common phenomenon in the works of Pierre Bourdieu, be it in "L'opinion publique n'existe pas" (1984) or in an interview published in 1984, entitled: "La 'jeunesse' n'est qu'un mot[34]" ('Youth is Just a Word'). In this, Pierre Bourdieu shares Rémi Lenoir's interest for different age categories and points out that the boundary existing between the young and the old is arbitrary: the two categories are not a given but they are socially constructed in the struggle between the "young" and the "old". Like his colleague, Bourdieu highlights the fact that "age is a socially manipulated and manipulable biological fact" and he further adds that "talking of the young as a social unit, a constituted group, with common interests and relating these interests to a biologically defined age, is in itself an obvious manipulation" (p. 145). According to Pierre Bourdieu, it is important to differentiate between young people based on their social origin because it inherently involves distinct lifestyles.

3. A NEW CONCEPT OF ACTION

The important sociological movements stand out essentially by the manner in which they foresee the actions carried out by individuals: while some, subjectivists, stress rationality or the liberty of social actors, others, objectivists, highlight the social determinisms that weigh on individuals. Based on his epistemological reflection, Pierre Bourdieu develops a new concept of action that tends to overcome the conventional oppositions of sociology, notably the opposition between objectivism and subjectivism.

3.1 Genetic Structuralism

Objectivism and Subjectivism

There are multiple oppositions in the field of social sciences (individualism/holism, micro/macro, individual/collective...). Among these oppositions, lies the opposition between subjectivism and objectivism. Subjectivism begins from representations and world views specific to individuals that form sociological knowledge. The advocates of objectivism, such as Émile Durkheim or Karl Marx, on the other hand, defend the idea that sociology should turn away from subjective representations of individuals (conceived as assumptions or ideologies) to focus on objective social structures which explain the functioning of society and which go beyond individual comprehension.

The principles of rupture and that of non-consciousness

places *Le Métier de Sociologue* (1968) in the objectivist tradition. However, the book is also a warning against the excesses of this position.

Questioning Structuralism and the Rejection of Subjectivism

The initial investigations of Pierre Bourdieu in Kabyle were influenced by the structuralism of the anthropologist Claude Lévi-Strauss. The latter was himself inspired by the research work of the linguist Ferdinand de Saussure who looked at language as a system in which the elements define themselves either by drawing a relation of equivalence or opposition with respect to the other elements. Claude Lévi-Strauss applied these principles to his object of study, the family. Kinship is thus analysed as a language which puts not only individuals but also families in relation with each other. Unconscious and universal rules, qualified as "invariable", govern these systems of kinship. The prohibition of incest, in particular, favours the movement of women within a social group. The analysis of objective structures thus seems to be inevitable in order to take stock of the social reality. In "La maison ou le monde renversé"[35] ("The Berber House or the World Reversed"), text published for the first time in 1969, Pierre Bourdieu turns to the structural analysis method by showing that the inner space of a household, feminine before anything else, structures itself by drawing a relation of inversion vis-a-vis the external space, which is above all masculine. Subsequently however, (especially after *Le Métier de sociologue*), he stresses more and more on the need to inquire into the meaning that agents assign to their practices in order to better understand the dialectic that exists between objective structures and integrated subjective structures. Without this, the sociologist is led to objectify, that is, consider as real, abstractions such as social classes or culture.

However, Pierre Bourdieu was always opposed to pure subjectivism. According to him, it is imperative to break away from spontaneous representations made by agents in order to construct a scientific discourse. The basis of his criticism of subjectivism lies in the questioning of the philosopher Jean-Paul Sartre's phenomenology. Sartre places emphasis on the liberty of individuals. He thinks that individuals are indeed capable of surmounting their objective situations by having recourse to the imaginary. As a result, the fact that individuals take stock of their actions by calling upon a certain determinism can be interpreted as a proof of "mauvaise foi" 'bad faith'. Pierre Bourdieu contests this concept of the freedom of the subject by affirming that social conditions of existence, that is, objective structures, remain at the centre of the explanation of individuals' behaviours. Using the same arguments, he opposes the theories of the rational actor that define the concept of predominant actions in economics. According to these theories, self-interest is the sole driving force behind actions and the actors are reduced to schemers who try to maximise their interests. Despite their conceptual distance, the phenomenology of Jean Paul Sartre and the theories of the rational actor are brought together par Pierre Bourdieu under the same label—that of "subjectivism"—to elucidate his own theory of action.

Surpassing the Opposition Between Objectivism and Subjectivism: Genetic Structuralism

After having discovered the paradoxes arrived at by objectivism on the one hand and by subjectivism on the other, Pierre Bourdieu expresses his willingness to go beyond the opposition between these two extremes. He thus states in *Choses dites*[36] (*In Other Words*): "If I liked the games with labels [..] I would say that I am trying to develop a genetic structuralism: the analysis of objective structures [..] is inseparable from the analysis of the genesis, within biological individuals, of the mental structures which are to some extent the product of the incorporation of social structures; inseparable, too, from the analysis of the genesis of these social structures themselves." (p. 24) "Genetic structuralism" which he describes in another text as "constructivist structuralism" or as "structuralist constructivism" (*Choses dites*, p. 147), thus makes the study of objective structures and that of subjective representations compatible, which, otherwise, seemed to be conflicting positions.

In a text entitled "Espace social et pouvoir symbolique"[37] ("Social Space and Symbolic Power"), Pierre Bourdieu explains the nature of genetic structuralism. According to him, surpassing the opposition between objectivism and subjectivism can only happen if the sociologist distinguishes between two fundamental moments in his research process. The objectivist break with ordinary language appears to be the first fundamental moment in research that brings to light the objective structures (which give a direction to subjective representations). However, the sociologist cannot stop at this first break and must, over a second phase, reintegrate the subjective world views which play a part in the construction of the social world. Pierre Bourdieu thereby explains: "On the one hand, the objective structures that the sociologist constructs, in the objectivist moment, by setting aside the subjective representations of the agents, form the basis for these representations and constitute the structural constraints that bear upon interactions; but, on the other hand, these representations must also be taken into consideration particularly if one wants to account for the daily struggles, individual and collective, which purport to transform or to preserve these structures" (p. 150).

3.2 The Notion of Habitus

History of the Notion

The notion of habitus, a central notion in Bourdieu's sociology, goes beyond the standard oppositions of sociology (objectivism / subjectivism, holism / individualism, macro / micro...). Although this notion was not invented by Pierre Bourdieu, the latter nevertheless redefines it, thus assuring it a place of importance within the ambit of conceptual sociological tools. Originally, the notion of habitus is a translation by Saint Thomas d'Aquinas, of the Aristotelian notion of *hexis*. Aristotle defines *hexis* as attitudes and corporal aptitudes (way to behave oneself, speech...) incorporated in education and which form an individual's current capacity for action. Saint Thomas d'Aquinas translates *hexis* as habitus and by that, he refers to the fact that socialisation inculcates practices, especially religious, that eventually become spontaneous. Thereafter, the notion of habitus is often re-employed but it still does not become a central element of any theory. When Pierre Bourdieu redefines habitus, he is inspired particularly by Aristotle, Saint Thomas d'Aquinas, Émile Durkheim, Norbert Elias, Marcel Mauss and Max Weber.

Definition of Habitus According to Pierre Bourdieu

Pierre Bourdieu has given multiple definitions of habitus. The most well-known definition is found in *Le Sens pratique*[38]: "The conditionings associated with a particular class of conditions of existence produce *habitus*, systems of durable, transposable *dispositions*, structured structures predisposed to function as structuring structures, that is, as principles which generate and organise practices and representations that can be objectively adapted to their outcomes without presupposing a conscious aiming at ends or an express mastery of the operations necessary in order to attain them (p. 88)

For Pierre Bourdieu, habitus is composed of frameworks of perception (ways of perceiving the world), of assessment (ways of judging it) and of action (ways of dealing with it) that have been internalised and embodied by individuals during the process of socialisation—infancy, during childhood, secondary education, in adulthood—in a more or less unconscious way. It is simultaneously composed of "mental structures through which [individuals] understand the world" (*Choses dites*, 1987) and of their corporal manifestations, referred to as corporal hexis taken from Aristotle.

Habitus vary according to the conditions of existence and the social trajectory of each individual. Since the conditions of existence are common to several people placed in the same socio-economic situation, these people share, in part, the same habitus. This allows Pierre Bourdieu to talk of class habitus (worker habitus or middle class habitus for instance). However, since each person has his own individual trajectory and occupies a particular position within his class, the habitus also consists of an individual dimension which implies that each particular habitus is seen as a variant of the collective habitus.

Habitus dispositions are durable to the extent that, being ingrained in people, they have a tendency to perpetuate and to resist any change. Except for radical changes in the conditions of the socio-economic environment, individuals tend to preserve the dispositions acquired during socialisation. Sometimes, when the social world changes but behaviours stemming from the habitus remain the same without adapting, it gives rise to the hysteresis effect. Hysteresis refers to the persistence of an effect while its cause has disappeared. In *Questions de sociologie* (1984), (*Sociology in Question*) Pierre Bourdieu cites the example of the novelist Cervantes' fictional character Don Quixote, who continues to behave like a knight in a world where knighthood no longer exists.

The dispositions that constitute the habitus are also referred to as "transposable". This means that the dispositions acquired in certain contexts (like in the family or at school) can be transposed to other contexts (for example at work, in the context of a sporting activity) which tend to create homogeneous "lifestyles".

Example: The Scholastic Habitus

Architecture gothique et pensée scolastique[39] (*Gothic Architecture and Scholasticism*), written by the German art historian Erwin Panofsky, is considered by Pierre Bourdieu —who translated the book into French and wrote an afterward in 1967—to be a confirmation of his theory of the habitus. In this book, Erwin Panofsky endeavours to understand the genesis of gothic architecture. He shows that the architects of gothic cathedrals, all trained by the scholastic school of thought (which monopolised education), transposed the principles of scholasticism into architecture. As a result, it is possible to observe a homology (that is, a structural similarity) between the scholastic thought (that claims to reconcile faith with reason by clarifying the article of faith as much as possible) and gothic architecture (open cathedrals, transparency, divisibility of structure). For Panofsky, this relationship was not coincidental : the structural similarity between scholastic thought and gothic architecture is not a matter of chance but the result of a causal relationship. Pierre Bourdieu interprets this equivalence in terms of the transposition of a habitus acquired in the course of school and religious education, into the professional and artistic domain.

3.3 Habitus and Practical Reason: From Actor to Agent

From Habitus to Practical Reason

Habitus thus comprises two dimensions. On the one hand, it is "the internalisation of externality": through the process of socialisation, it allows for the "internalisation of structures belonging to the social world" (*Choses dites*, 1987), in other words, it is the internalisation of the boundaries within which it is possible to act. On the other hand, habitus simultaneously allows for an "externalisation of internality" owing to its role of a "structuring structure" that generates practices. In reality, habitus enables individuals, in a certain given situation, to produce a behaviour that corresponds to what is expected of them by the social context (that is, to match the subjective structures with objective structures of the social world) without having to necessarily reflect upon them, owing to the fact that they have already internalised the externality of the social world.

This ability to know how to behave in a given situation, without prior reflection, on account of it being formerly internalised unconsciously in the past, is at the heart of practical reason. Pierre Bourdieu uses the example of the tennis player to illustrate the notion of practical reason. The tennis player anticipates the area where the ball will fall without any prior reflection. His practical mastery of the game saves him from thinking before every shot. Practical reason, a product of habitus, allows to save reflection time during action.

Opposition to the Theory of the Rational Actor: From Actor to Agent

The notion of practical reason directly opposes the theory of the rational actor: according to this theory the actions of individuals are always motivated by a rational calculation akin to a cost-benefit analysis. Pierre Bourdieu, with the help of the habitus and the notion of practical reason, shows that it is possible to objectively achieve behaviours that serve a purpose without them being products of any calculation. The tennis player finds himself de facto at the right spot to tackle the ball without having to elaborate a theory or to define the reason for his action before every shot.

Pierre Bourdieu dismissed the concept of a rational actor in order to introduce the idea that behaviours are in part the product of habitus that represents the incorporated social element. In doing so, he decided to change the vocabulary: rather than speaking of the actor, he spoke of the agent. In fact, the notion of the agent enabled to reconcile two dimensions: on the one hand, the agent is the one that acts (outwards) and on the other hand, he is also the one who is acted upon (from inside, as a result of his habitus).

Evolution of the Notion of Habitus

Pierre Bourdieu's concept of action was sharply criticised. The sociologist was especially reproached for being excessively deterministic when he considered agents as "cultural idiots"[40] who are completely subjugated by their habitus and as a result are devoid of reflexivity at the time of action.

Pierre Bourdieu's concept of habitus is however not as simplistic as it appears. It has evolved and it has been redefined during the course of the sociologist's researches. Although initially it appears to be a notion that reconciles liberty and determinism, the notion of habitus, in the initial formulation (*La Reproduction*[41]) inclines towards determinism. It propounds the idea that subjective structures of individuals are externally determined by the objective structures of the social world. This renders the actions of the social agents predictable. On the other hand, in the second formulation of habitus the possibility of invention by the actors is left open. In doing so, it reduces the predictability of their behaviours by stressing on the generative capacity of the habitus: "But then why not say habit? Habit is spontaneously regarded as repetitive, mechanical, automatic, reproductive rather than productive. I wanted to insist on the idea that habitus is something that is powerfully generative. To put it briefly, habitus is a product of conditionings which tends to reproduce the objective logic of those conditionings while transforming it. It's a kind of transforming machine that leads us to 'reproduce' the social conditions of our own production, but in a relatively unpredictable way, in such a way that one cannot move simply and mechanically from knowledge of the conditions of production to knowledge of the products." (*Questions de sociologie*, pp. 134-135)

NOTES

1. *Le Bal des célibataires. Crise de la société paysanne en Béarn* (2002), Paris, Le Seuil.
2. *Sociologie de l'Algérie* (1958), *Paris, Presses Universitaires de France.*
3. Bourdieu, P., Darbel A., Rivet J.-P. et Seibel C., *Travail et travailleurs en Algérie* (1963), Paris, Mouton.
4. Bourdieu, P. et Sayad A., Le Déracinement. *La Crise de l'agriculture traditionnelle en Algérie* (1964), Paris, Minuit.
5. *Esquisse d'une théorie de la pratique* (1972), Genève, Droz.
6. *Le Sens pratique* (1980), Paris, Minuit.
7. *La Domination masculine* (1998), Paris, Le Seuil.
8. Bourdieu, P., Passeron J.-C., *Les Héritiers. Les étudiants et la culture* (1964), Paris, Minuit.
9. Bourdieu, P. (dir.), *Un Art moyen. Essai sur les usages sociaux de la photographie* (1965), Paris, Minuit.
10. Bourdieu, P. (dir.), *L'Amour de l'art. Les musées d'art européens et leur public* (1966), Paris, Minuit.
11. *Les Règles de l'art. Genèse et structure du champ littéraire* (1992), Paris, Seuil.

12. Bourdieu, P., Chamboredon J.-C., Passeron, J.-C., *Le Métier de sociologue: préalables épis- témologiques* (1968), Paris, Mouton.
13. Bourdieu, P., Passeron, J.-C., *La Reproduction. Eléments pour une théorie du système d'enseignement* (1970), Paris, Minuit.
14. *La Distinction. Critique sociale du jugement* (1979), Paris, Minuit.
15. Bourdieu, P. (dir.), *La Misère du monde* (1993), Paris, Le Seuil.
16. *Contre-feux 1. Propos pour servir à la résistance contre l'invasion néo-libérale* (1998), Paris, Raisons d'agir.
17. *Contre-feux 2. Pour un mouvement social européen* (2001), Paris, Raisons d'agir.
18. *Sur la télévision, suivi de L'Emprise du journalisme* (1996), Paris, Raisons d'agir.
19. Carles, P., *La sociologie est un sport de combat* (2001), Buena Vista Home Entertainement.
20. *Méditations pascaliennes* (1997), Paris, Le Seuil.
21. *Science de la science et réflexivité. Cours du Collège de France 2000-2001* (2001), Paris, Raisons d'agir.
22. Bourdieu, P., Chamboredon, J.-C., Passeron, J.-C., *Le Métier de sociologue: préalables épis- témologiques* (1968), Paris, Mouton.
23. Durkheim, É., *Les Règles de la méthode sociologique* (1895), Paris, Presses Universitaires de France.
24. *Questions de sociologie* (1984), Paris, Minuit, p. 19.
25. Durkheim, É., *Le Suicide. Étude de sociologie* (1897), Paris, Presses Universitaires de France.
26. Passeron, J.-C., *Le Raisonnement sociologique. L'espace non-poppérien du raisonnement natu- rel* (2006, [1991]), Paris, Nathan.
27. *Questions de sociologie* (1984), Paris, Minuit, p. 19.
28. "L'opinion publique n'existe pas", *in Questions de sociologie* (1984), Paris, Minuit, pp. 222-234.
29. "L'illusion biographique", *in Raisons pratiques. Sur la théorie de l'action* (1994), Paris, Seuil, pp. 81-89.
30. Bourdieu, P. (dir.), *La Misère du monde* (1993), Paris, Seuil.
31. The social impoverishment highlighted in the book is more about the "poverty of position" than the "poverty of condition". In other words, less emphasis is placed on the dilapidated physical conditions as compared to the legitimate aspirations that individuals give up due to their position in the social space.

32. *Esquisse pour une auto-analyse* (2004), Paris, Raisons d'agir.
33. "L'invention du troisième âge. Constitution du champ des agents de gestion de la vieillesse", *Actes de la recherche en sciences sociales* (1979), Nos. 26-27, pp. 57-82.
34. "La "jeunesse" n'est qu'un mot", in *Questions de sociologie* (1984), Paris, Minuit, pp. 143-154.
35. "La maison ou le monde renversé", in *Esquisse d'une théorie de la pratique* (1972), Genève, Droz, pp. 61-82.
36. *Choses dites* (1987), Paris, Minuit.
37. "Espace social et pouvoir symbolique", in *Choses dites* (1987), Paris, Minuit, pp. 147- 166.
38. *Le Sens pratique* (1980), Paris, Minuit.
39. Panofsky, E., *Architecture gothique et pensée scolastique* (1967, [1951]), Paris, Minuit.
40. Garfinkel, H., *Studies in Ethnomethodology* (1967), Englewood Cliffs, Prentice-Hall. Harold Garfinkel parle de "cultural dopes".
41. Bourdieu, P., Passeron, J.-C., *La Reproduction. Éléments pour une théorie du système d'ensei- gnement* (1970), Paris, Minuit.

2

Sociology of Education

The initial groundwork of a sociology of education had been done at the beginning of the twentieth century, by Emile Durkheim in *L'Évolution pédagogique en France (1904-1905)*[42] (*The Pedagogical Evolution in France*). In this analysis, he considers the school to be a form of socialisation whose function it is to encourage social integration, while inculcating in each individual the moral values that form the foundation of society. In doing so, the school liberates individuals from their distinctive family traits while ensuring that social order is maintained.

After Emile Durkheim and up to the works of Pierre Bourdieu and Jean-Claude Passeron in the 1960s, very few sociologists tackled the question of education. In fact, during the first half of the twentieth century, education was not even an active domain of sociological study in France. Between 1950-1960, the legitimate objects of sociological study in France comprised of the workplace (Georges Friedmann), the working class (Paul-Henri Chombart de Lauwe), the bureaucracy (Michel Crozier), religion (Hervé Le Bras), the city (Henri Lefevre), the peasantry (Henri Mendras), leisure time (Jean Dumazedier) as well as social psychology (Georges Gurvitch, Jean Stoetzel).

Ever since the 1960s, there has been a recently developed eagerness and a renewed interest among sociologists regarding the question of education. While the number of students going to secondary school and to university remained stable throughout the first half of the twentieth century, it rose exponentially during the *baby boom* period, with the birth of children after the war. This rise in the number of students led to the opening of educational institutions to cater to newer populations and also led to a prolongation of education through institutional reforms that aimed to better train students in order to face the new social and economic conditions. Thus, since 1959, the Berthoin decree made schooling compulsory for children between 14 to 16 years, and in 1963, the Fouchet decree removed entrance examinations for entry into middle school and established the Collèges d'Enseignement Général. This was a prelude to the Haby reform of 1975 that created the collège unique. At the same time, thanks to the rise in the standard of living, people nursed hopes of upward social mobility for their children through schools. This new dimension of schooling institutions described as "massification", is interpreted as democratisation: henceforth, all individuals, irrespective of their social origin, would have equal opportunities of access to education and certifications that these institutions confer. The works of Pierre Bourdieu and Jean-Claude Passeron however countered this interpretation, by highlighting the obstacles that prevent massification from transforming into democratisation.

1. THE SCHOOL AS AN EXAMPLE OF SOCIAL REPRODUCTION

Pierre Bourdieu's research on schooling profoundly reformed the sociology of education in the 1960s. These research works were also opportunities for Pierre Bourdieu to devise and test a few of his major concepts that define sociology today (habitus, cultural capital, symbolic violence).

Three principle books construct Pierre Bourdieu's thesis

on the sociology of education: *Les Héritiers. Les étudiants et la culture*[43], *La Reproduction. Éléments pour une théorie du système d'enseignement*[44], et *La Noblesse d'État. Grandes écoles et esprit de corps*[45]. The first two books were written with Jean-Claude Passeron, the third book was written in collaboration with Monique de Saint-Martin. *Les Héritiers* is written in the form of an essay that develops the main ideas that are revisited and theorised in *La Reproduction*. In *La Noblesse d'État*, while still using the arguments of the two previous works, the book focused less on universities and more on the *Grandes Écoles*, which are highly selective, elite, and prestigious higher education institutions. Pierre Bourdieu's sociology of education essentially deals with higher education.

If one were to condense his concept in one sentence, the theory propounded in these books could be stated like so: rather than favouring equal opportunities, the school contributes to the reproduction of social inequalities and legitimises these inequalities by using a meritocratic discourse. Although, like Emile Durkheim, Pierre Bourdieu considers the school to be a central institution in contemporary societies, he however breaks with Durkheim's positive vision of the school as the purveyor of moral norms and adopts, on the contrary, a critical stance.

1.1 From Social Inequalities to Educational Inequalities

The Statistical Assessment: Differences in Academic Success Based on Social Origin

Drafted in the context of the 1960s, a period which was favourable to the import of American quantitative techniques (those elaborated particularly by Paul Lazaresfeld), the book *Les Héritiers* (1964) leads to a certain number of statistical results stemming from questionnaire-based surveys carried out by Pierre Bourdieu, Jean-Claude

Passeron and their team members in the CSE (Centre de sociologie européenne). The statistician Alain Darbel did a groundbreaking analysis through the use of the conditional probabilities method which compares the relative chances of academic success based on social origin, gender, place of residence, etc.

Statistical analysis highlights the importance of social origin, which acts as a differentiating factor, when it comes to gaining access to higher education: "The son of a senior executive is eighty times more likely to enter a university than a farm worker's son, and forty times more likely than an industrial worker's son; and he is twice as likely to enter a university than a lower-rank executive's son" (p. 12). In addition to this "elimination" phenomenon, there are two other types of educational inequalities that have been studied: "relegation" to less prestigious fields (arts and sciences as opposed to law and medicine) and "delay or stalling", which means grade repetition before or during higher studies. In all the three cases, social origin appears to be the most decisive differentiating factor: it has a stronger impact than gender (although relegation also seems to be a gender-based inequality), age or even religious affiliation. Children coming from working classes are the most affected by elimination, relegation and late arrival.

The Cultural Advantage of the Most Privileged Social Categories with Regard to School

According to Pierre Bourdieu and Jean-Claude Passeron, social inequalities affecting academic success are not so much a result of a difference in wealth as it is of cultural differences. At this point, both the authors move away from the classical Marxist analysis. They show that "the more privileged the social origin of students, the richer, wider and more varied their knowledge" (*Les Héritiers*, p. 30).

"Cultural privilege" is characteristic of students coming from the most affluent classes. In *La Reproduction* (1970), the authors introduce the notion of "cultural capital" to describe the knowledge and ability to appreciate different cultural forms originating from the "high culture", which is the culture valued by cultural institutions (theatre, classical music, painting, etc.). This cultural capital is more significant for affluent social classes. The cultural privilege of students coming from affluent categories with respect to education can be defined as the proximity between the culture that they have acquired from their social and family environments and the culture in school. The latter values the same works as the learned society. Conversely, students belonging to the most disadvantaged sections of society do not possess, as a consequence of their family socialisation, the cultural skills valued by the school. In fact, different social classes are distinguished by their "unequal distances with respect to the academic culture and their different abilities to recognise and acquire them" (*La Reproduction*, p. 128).

The differentiated relationship to culture based on social origin is evident even when it comes to the language spoken. Pierre Bourdieu and Jean-Claude Passeron refer to the works of the sociolinguist Basil Bernstein ("Social Structure, Language and Learning"[46]) to demonstrate that "academic success closely depends on the aptitude (real or perceived) to use the language of ideas that is particular to education" (*Les Héritiers*, p. 25). According to Basil Bernstein, the language spoken by the upper classes is a formal and elaborate language that corresponds to the linguistic codes used in schools. Conversely, the language spoken by the working classes, considered to be ordinary or restricted, is characterised by a limited vocabulary and a finite range of possibilities for structuring a speech. Unable to master the elaborated codes used in school, students belonging to weaker social sections thus find themselves at a disadvantageous position. Henceforth, the language spoken is taken to be a source of academic inequality.

Depending on their social group, the students do not have the same resources at their disposal that can help them adapt to the academic culture. In *Les Héritiers*, Pierre Bourdieu and Jean-Claude Passeron distinguish between three social classes and they analyse their differentiated relationships with the academic culture. The cultural advantage enjoyed by the privileged social categories allows students, coming from that background, to maintain an independent and neutral relationship with the academic culture: "Thus the ironic casualness, mannered elegance, or the statutory assurance which lends ease or the affectation of ease are almost always the mark of students from the upper classes, where such manners signal membership in the elite." (34). For children of peasants, industrial workers, clerks or small shopkeepers who are removed from the high culture of the elite that is valued in schools, "the acquisition of academic culture is acculturation" (p. 37) which means that it implies a detachment from one's own cultural background in order to better absorb the scholastic norms and values. The middle class is ultimately characterised not so much by its great ability to assimilate the scholastic culture but by its greater propensity to acquire it. A "cultural willingness", based on complete adhesion to scholastic values, is thus transmitted to families belonging to the lower middle class who aspire for social mobility through academic success (the objective probability is weak but real). Owing to its proximity to high culture, the scholastic culture, that facilitates the dilettantism of the cultivated classes, is laboriously acquired by members of the other social groups. "For some, the learning of elite culture is a conquest paid for in effort; for others, it is a heritage, which implies both facility and the temptations of facility." (p. 40)

The notion of habitus, introduced in *La Reproduction* (the authors had spoken of "cultural habitus" in *Les Héritiers*), helps to theorise the relationship of the different classes with culture. Thus the habitus that the school aims to inculcate is more or less similar to the habitus inculcated by the family within the social milieu or the class habitus which is characterised by frameworks of perceptions and considerations that are common to a certain social class. The greater the distance between the two habitus, the lesser the chances of scholastic success. As a result, members of the lower classes, owing to their class habitus, tend to auto-eliminate themselves in advance from secondary or higher education by assuming that studies are not meant for them. This also shows that class inequality is more likely to be the reason behind this auto-elimination rather than scholastic failure. It is as if the most disadvantaged groups had internalised their objectively weak probability of having access to higher education into their habitus and they modify their behaviour according to their objective probability of success.

A Differentiated Relation to Studies Based on Social Origin

In *Les Héritiers*, Pierre Bourdieu and Jean-Claude Passeron examine the unity of the student circle. According to them, if students are characterised by their common practices (university assignments, class hours, exams, etc.), they do not live their student life in the same way owing to their social backgrounds. Nevertheless, they all reinterpret the relation that they have with social backgrounds according to the models of the intellectual class to which they aspire. As intellectual learners, they try, in particular, to prevent the influence of their family backgrounds from being apprehended and identify with their professors who they consider to be "thought leaders and life coaches". In the 1960s, the students of the faculty of arts in Paris represented, according to the authors, the "*typical-ideal* image"[47] of these intellectual learners. Their bourgeois origins predispose them to easily adopt the codes of the intellectual class as compared to the others.

If studies are a means to equip students for their future, students however tend to consider the duration of learning as an end in itself. By making references to the figure of the "eternal apprentice", they maintain a mystified relationship with their studies: the authors describe them as the "sorcerer's apprentice". However not all students are able to partake of this mystification. Students belonging to the most disadvantaged sections of society, reeling under economic obligations, adopt a more realistic view of education since their future is directly affected by their academic success: they are thus compelled to remain simple "apprentices" and choose disciplines that are sure to provide them with employment (the arts, for instance, are streams that are excluded). Depending on their class habitus, students are thus more or less similar to the established figure of the student.

The Role of the School in the Production of Inequalities

Pierre Bourdieu and Jean-Claude Passeron question the republican belief in meritocracy which states that the school promotes equal opportunities. In reality, the idea of formal equality amongst students only renders educational institutions unmindful of real inequalities that actually exist. Indeed schools treat all students equally when it comes to culture, even though they are de facto unequal: schools thus demonstrate an "indifference to differences" (*La Reproduction*, p. 220). The problem lies in the fact that by refusing to establish a link between the social origin of students and the level of their cultural capital, schools reinforce a system of differential selection based on the social background. For example, in a competition or an exam, the test papers and qualifying requirements remain the same for all the candidates: on the outside, the competition or the exam gives equal opportunities to every candidate, but this would mean "forgetting that the formal equality provided by the competitive examination merely transforms the social privilege into merit, since it allows the influence of social origin to operate, through more secret channels" (*Les Héritiers*, p. 104).

In the hope of evaluating all the students on an equal footing, the school views social differences as mere scholastic differences, thus transforming social hierarchy into scholastic ranking. This ignorance on behalf of the school and the reinforcement of inequalities that results from it, can be summarised in the following manner: "So that the privileged classes are favoured even more and the underprivileged are discriminated against, it is necessary and sufficient for the school to ignore the cultural inequalities that exist between children of different social classes with respect to the content of instruction delivered, the methods and techniques of instruction, and the assessment criteria."[48]

In order to justify the unequal academic results, the school attributes them to differences in the natural abilities of the students. In doing so, they foster an "ideology of gift", a "charismatic ideology", which passes off successful academic performances as innate abilities. On the other hand, Pierre Bourdieu and Jean-Claude Passeron showed that these abilities were in fact cultural and were acquired within the social and family environment. In *La Reproduction*, the authors analyse, for instance, the remark made to certain students for being "too pedantic", which, coming from the school, is a paradoxical reproach. This criticism, formulated as a judgement on the natural personal ability of students, recognises in reality, a social difference which indicates a distinctive feature peculiar to the lower middle classes who fail to acquire the high culture (or "free culture") that is valued by the school and are thus forced to make visible efforts in order to succeed. In the same way, positive assessments and good results are attributed to the personal merit of the student even though they point towards a social proximity to the scholastic culture. The ideology of gift eventually enables the educational institution to legitimise the classification that it establishes amongst students on the grounds of meritocracy. By portraying itself as a meritocratic institution, the school legitimises its functioning. In doing so, under the guise of equality of opportunities, the school transforms social heritage into academic merit. A lack of knowledge about how the institution really works reinforces people's belief in the validity of the ideology of gift. In fact, the very efficiency of this ideology is due to the fact that it is universally accepted.

An Alternative Individualistic Explanation of the Inequality of Opportunities: Raymond Boudon

French sociologist and proponent of methodological individualism, Raymond Boudon, is opposed to the sociology of Pierre Bourdieu which is built on the structural theory and is thus rather objectivist. Boudon prefers a concept of action that underlines the rationality of actors' behaviours. Considering that objective structures that could transcend individuals' actions do not exist, Raymond Boudon proposes to re-establish the motives or the "right reasons" that influence actors who are defined by their individualities, in order to explain micro sociological phenomena. In his opinion, the social regularities that are recorded are nothing but "statistical traces left by the juxtaposition of a myriad of individual behaviours."[49] In his book *L'Inégalité des chances. La mobilité sociale dans les sociétés industrielles,*[50] Boudon criticises the theories developed in *Les Héritiers* and *La Reproduction.* He attacks their determinism and offers an alternative explanation of inequality of opportunities.

According to Raymond Boudon, the inequality of academic opportunities is a result of the confluence of social positions and "points of bifurcation", i.e. orientation stages that delineate the academic institution. At each stage, the academic direction (the pursuit or non-pursuit of studies, long-term or short-term studies, technical subjects or non-specialised courses, etc.) is taken depending on the perception, of the student and that of his family, of his chances for success. The student's academic potential is crucial in the evaluation of his chances for success. Nevertheless, his social position also determines, to a certain extent, his decisions about his academic orientation: the probability of renouncing the pursuit of studies is higher as one goes down the social hierarchy. Raymond Boudon highlights the phenomenon of auto-selection: children coming from modest backgrounds, who are equally competent in their studies, resort to self-censorship and tend to choose short-term courses. The sociologist explains this academic choice through a cost-benefit calculation that is done by the student and his family: they make this decision based on the return they expect from their educational investment. This return appears to be lower for poorer backgrounds due to the greater economic and cultural distance that need to be covered in order to attain faster social mobility.

The auto-selection phenomenon had already been underlined by Pierre Bourdieu and Jean-Claude Passeron who spoke of "auto-elimination" of underprivileged social groups in *La Reproduction.* However, the definition of this phenomenon differs according to the sociological perspective adopted. While Pierre Bourdieu et Jean-Claude Passeron consider that the habitus of the lower classes, which is removed from the scholastic culture, is the reason behind their anticipation of failure, Raymond Boudon refers to a cost-benefit calculation in order to explain their academic choices.

1.2 From Educational Inequalities to Social Inequalities

From Cultural Reproduction to Social Reproduction

In contemporary societies, social hierarchy is modelled on scholastic hierarchy. The degrees and diplomas awarded by the school places the individual in a distinctive position in society. Pierre Bourdieu demonstrates, in particular, that studying in prestigious institutions (École nationale d'administration, Polytechnique) is the gateway to the most respectable posts.

The ideology of gift disseminated by the school, which states that the difference in scholastic success can be completely attributed to individual merit and ability, legitimises the social position occupied at the end of education. The discourse on meritocracy enables the legitimisation of not only scholastic hierarchy but also social hierarchy which stems from it. The school thus appears to be an authority that can control and enshrine at the same time.

According to Pierre Bourdieu and Jean-Claude Passeron, the meritocratic discourse promoted by the school is nothing but an "ideology" and the legitimised social order does not correspond to actual meritocracy. The selection and classification is done by the school on the basis of the greater or lesser proximity of the students to the academic culture, which has great proximity to the elite culture. Thus, scholastic hierarchy is not a reflection of the personal abilities of students but of the fundamental social inequalities. Social inequalities that become scholastic inequalities transform back into social inequalities at the end of education. The school is thus portrayed by Pierre Bourdieu and Jean-Claude Passeron (*La Reproduction*, 1970) as an instance of social reproduction.

The school finally appears to be the "black box" that transforms a social hierarchy, that is illegitimate since it depends on family heritage, into a relatively identical social hierarchy that is legitimised by academic qualifications which are supposedly awarded on the basis of personal merits. The charismatic ideology of gift thus plays a central role in the legitimisation of social reproduction that is no longer viewed as reproduction.

Nevertheless, the reproduction carried out by the school is not an exact reflection of the prior classification of social positions. In fact, the educational system has a relative but real autonomy in relation to the elite class and its culture, which allows it to set its own classification criteria. The distance, small but real, between the academic culture and the high culture leads to a relative blurring between social hierarchy and scholastic hierarchy. This blurring of boundaries empowers the school to assert complete autonomy vis-a-vis the social structure, even though it is incapable of questioning the cultural disparity that exists between social groups.

Domination and Symbolic Violence

The social space, according to Pierre Bourdieu, is a space that is polarised between the dominant, which comprises of the higher classes, and the dominated, represented by the underprivileged classes. By ensuring the reproduction of this social structure, the school reinforces the domination (cultural, social, economic...) by the dominant classes. The understanding of the phenomenon of domination constitutes the subject of an important work of sociological theorisation by Pierre Bourdieu.

Pierre Bourdieu borrows the notion of "domination" from the German sociologist Max Weber who defines it as: "the probability that certain specific commands [..] will be obeyed by a specified group of people."[51] He distinguishes the notion of "domination" from that of "ability" or "power" which is defined by Weber as "the chance to assert one's will within a network of social relations, even against the resistance of others" (p. 95). While power is realised only through coercion, domination requires "a minimum level of willingness to obey" by those who are subjected to it. Pierre Bourdieu revisits the questions asked by Max Weber, in order to examine the origin of domination, its sustainability and its functioning mechanism.

In *La Reproduction*, Pierre Bourdieu and Jean-Claude Passeron introduce the expression "symbolic violence" which eventually becomes a central theme in the Bourdieusian framework. The first part of the book is thus called "Foundations of a theory of symbolic violence" and begins as follows: "The power to exert symbolic violence, i.e. any power which manages to impose meanings and to impose them as legitimate by concealing the power relations which are the basis of its force, adds its own specifically symbolic force to those power relations." (p. 18). The authors further add that "all pedagogic action (PA) is, objectively, symbolic violence insofar as it is the imposition of a cultural arbitrary by an arbitrary power." (p. 19). The school practises symbolic violence when it universally imposes a "cultural arbitrary". By prioritising the culture of the elite, it imposes it on all the students as the only legitimate culture. By doing so, it legitimises the existing power relations between the social classes, while concealing at the same time, through the dissemination of the ideology of gift, the existence of these power relations and the mechanisms of reproduction that are at work. This results in the natural acceptance of academic failure, which is portrayed to be due to a lack of merit rather than as a problem of distance from the scholastic culture. The imposition of an arbitrary culture by the school leads to the elimination (legitimised) of the dominated who are not able to reach the top of the scholastic hierarchy nor that of the social hierarchy.

To exercise domination, symbolic violence assumes the consent of the dominated as well as the dominant. The "willingness to obey" by those who are subjected to domination, in the words of Max Weber, can be explained, according to Pierre Bourdieu, as a universal adherence to a set of beliefs. Amongst these beliefs exists the ideology of gift promulgated by the school which benefits the dominant classes. The integration of this ideology contributes to the internalisation of the power relations between the social classes.

The mechanisms of domination and of symbolic violence are not restricted only to the area of education. They are seen in every sphere of the social world. Pierre Bourdieu's study on *La Domination masculine*[52] (*Masculine Domination*) brings to light the functioning of these mechanisms in the domestic sphere. In this book, Bourdieu examines the conditions that favour the continued domination of men over women. The reproduction of this domination relies on the acquisition, depending on the gender, of either a masculine habitus (or "virile habitus") or a feminine habitus. Masculine domination is thus incorporated into men as well as into women. It continues to persist through symbolic violence, which it produces, by persuading women to approve of this domination: "Symbolic violence is established by means of an adherence that the dominated cannot fail to grant to the dominant (and therefore to the domination), as she does not have at her disposal, to shape her thoughts and to think of herself or to reflect on her relation with the dominant, anything better than instruments of knowledge that she shares with the dominant, which, being no more than the embodied form of the relation of domination, causes the relationship to appear as natural" (p. 55). The women, victims of such symbolic domination, are therefore compelled to perceive the world through a system of "masculine" representation. Consequently, they take part in their own domination. Pierre Bourdieu cites the example of a large majority of French women who prefer partners who are taller than them, showing a clear preference for more dominant partners, in terms of their height. This compliance to the principle of domination, stemming from the acquisition of a specific habitus, is defined as "*amor fati*, love of one's social destiny" (p. 58). L'*amor fati*, relevant to women as well as to other underprivileged social categories, consists of "an unconscious adjustment to the probabilities associated with an objective structure of domination" (p. 58). Dropping out of the educational system, which is characteristic of the lower classes who think that long-term studies are not meant for them, can be interpreted as a form of *amor fati*. It is because of this principle that the differences in social destinies are perceived to be natural. The task of the sociologist is, therefore, to reveal the mechanisms that naturalise these differences through a "historical work of dehistoricisation" (p. 114). According to Pierre Bourdieu, the structures of domination are indeed "*the product of an incessant (and therefore historical) labour of reproduction*, to which singular agents (including men (...)) and institutions —families, the church, the school, the state-contribute (p. 55).

The School, an Important Example of Reproduction in Contemporary Societies

Pierre Bourdieu's sociology comes across, above all else, as a sociology of reproduction. In his article "Stratégies de reproduction et modes de domination"[53] (Strategies of Reproduction and Modes of Domination), Pierre Bourdieu writes that, "one of the most fundamental questions concerning the social world is the question of knowing how and why the world goes on, perseveres in being, how the social order perpetuates, that is the ordered set of relations that constitute it" (p. 3).

The school has not always been the principal instrument of social reproduction. In his article in 1994, Pierre Bourdieu explains that, in pre-capitalist societies, matrimonial strategies were predominant compared to scholastic strategies. Pre-capitalist societies were characterised by a mode of reproduction that was essentially familial in which matrimonial strategies, in order to avoid an unsuitable match (marriage with a person of a lower class in the social hierarchy), participated in the upholding of the social status.

The emergence of the state led to a transformation in the strategies of reproduction. As the modes of domination becomes impersonal, the reproduction of the social order relies increasingly on the structures of the state, especially on educational institutions. The diploma has a new function: from being a simple statutory attribute, it has become a real entitlement to admission. The privileged classes subsequently need to convert their cultural capital to scholastic capital in order to legitimise their dominant position within the social structure. In fact, the family "loses control over its successional decision as well as the power to designate an heir" (p. 10), this power being henceforth incumbent upon the school.

Although predominant, the strategies of academic

reproduction are however not the only strategies of reproduction at work in contemporary societies. In the "système de stratégies de reproduction" (p. 8) (System of Reproduction Strategies) which characterises all human society, they have not completely replaced the matrimonial strategies which exist especially in families that own companies. Thus Pierre Bourdieu warns against an evolutionist vision which places the school in succession to the family as a means of reproduction: "It is rather a question of the difference between a purely familial management of the problems of reproduction and a family owned business that introduces certain functions of the school in its strategies of reproduction." (p. 10) The family thus preserves its role in social reproduction, even if only through the transmission, within the household, of cultural capital and academic orientation decisions.

Pierre Bourdieu's article (1994) brings us to the notion of "strategy", which is a central notion in his entire work. He writes in a footnote: "Breaking with the dominant use of the notion, which considers strategies to be long-term conscious goals of an individual agent, I used this term to talk of a set of organised actions in anticipation of more or less long-term goals and not necessarily laid out as such, that are produced by the members of a collectivity" (p. 4). Strategy does not stem, according to Pierre Bourdieu, from an individual cost-benefit calculation as stated by the advocates of methodological individualism. Even though it is defined as the pursuit of goals, the agents who employ it are not necessarily conscious of the fact. Thus, «strategies of reproduction do not have, in principle, a conscious and rational intention, but rather dispositions of the habitus that tend to spontaneously reproduce the conditions of its own production" (p. 6). Habitus and not rational calculation, is the principle behind the strategies that are implemented.

1.3 From Academic Controversy to Public Debate

The Question of Democratisation

Is massification of education, that is to say gaining access to education by a greater majority, sufficient to ensure the democratisation of education, which means providing every individual equal prospects for academic success irrespective of his social origin? In his article "Classement, déclassement, reclassement"[54] (Classification, Declassification, Reclassification), Pierre Bourdieu addresses this question in an unequivocal manner: according to him, instead of promoting democratisation, massification of education leads to the establishment of new mechanisms that favour social reproduction. Before the massification of education, only a few specific social categories like intellectual professions, engineers ... required degrees to occupy their social position. The necessity to have an academic certification to occupy job positions, which earlier, did not require graduating from an educational institution (company owners, craftspersons, traders) and the education of girls have boosted the demand for education (massification). The latter has even led to an intensification of competition for academic credentials. Since the increase in the number of jobs, which require educational certifications, has been slower than the increase in demand for degrees, it has resulted in a credential inflation. This phenomenon has had two consequences: on one hand, awarding academic credentials has led to their devaluation and, on the other hand, non-graduates have been marginalised in a society where academic degrees are a general norm. Thus, contrary to popular belief, the massification of education has not improved the situation of the most deprived groups. It has instead resulted in a declassification of non-graduates as well as of graduates whose academic credentials are losing their value.

Far from promoting democratisation, the massification of education, in Bourdieu's opinion, contributes instead to the reproduction of the social order. In fact, it brings about a "global displacement in the structure of distribution among classes or fractions of classes" (p. 19), "a simple vertical displacement and not a real distortion" (p. 20) of the social structure.

Bourdieusian sociology makes a rather pessimistic observation of the role of the school, which is perceived to be an institution of social reproduction. Nevertheless, in his books co-authored with Jean-Claude Passeron, Bourdieu outlined possible solutions for the genuine democratisation of education. Firstly, sociology itself is a means of bringing about change, as it exposes the ideology of gift, which is at the root of the domination and whose force lies in its invisibility. Secondly, to democratise education, it is necessary for professors to "spill the beans", that is, clearly state their requirements and techniques that are needed to succeed, thus making the evaluation system more transparent. The rationalisation of education "in keeping with the interests of the most disadvantage students" can be implemented after reflecting on different pedagogical methods (lectures, tutorials, seminars...), on their content and on the pedagogical relationship established with the students depending on their social backgrounds. Despite these recommendations, at times criticised for being too theoretical, the Bourdieusian sociology on education has often been perceived to be fatalistic.

By blaming the school, viewed earlier as an instrument of democratisation and meritocracy, for being an instrument that promotes the reproduction of privileges, Pierre Bourdieu puts a check on hopes of upward social mobility with the help of the school. He has been criticised for replacing a biological determinism (talent) by a social determinism (habitus), thus depriving people of their power of resistance against the system. In 1970, Antoine Prost published, in the journal *Esprit*, an article entitled "Une sociologie stérile, la reproduction"[55] (Reproduction, a Sterile Sociology), where he accused Pierre Bourdieu of nihilism due to the demotivating nature of his sociology. However, not all researchers are as critical of the Bourdieusian corpus which has considerably influenced later researches on the sociology of education.

Pierre Bourdieu's theory is widely discussed even outside academic circles. A distinctive feature of the works of Pierre Bourdieu and Jean-Claude Passeron is that its far-reaching impact extends beyond the sociological world. The critique of the functioning of the world of education found favourable political and social conditions in the May 1968 movement. More than the mechanism of reproduction, it is the denunciation of traditional pedagogical practices and their consequences leading to academic inequalities that gained ground among student unions and left-wing political parties: criticism of the "lycées casernes" (high schools that looked and felt like prisons and military barracks), the arbitrariness of the academic culture, lectures and the discretionary power of teachers.

The success of these works can also be attributed to their convergence with the criticism of the republican school system, formulated since the beginning of the twentieth century, by pedagogues who denounced the social elitism existing in schools and in their teaching methods. Pierre Bourdieu and Jean-Claude Passeron's criticism of this system is twice as potent. On the one hand, their arguments are not limited to an analysis of pedagogical practices that underestimate the influence of the society on the functioning of the school. On the other hand, they avoid a Marxist analysis that reduces conflicts to an economic struggle while turning a blind eye to the symbolic dimension. The latter was specifically directed towards Christian Baudelot and Roger Establet, authors of *L'École capitaliste en France*[56] (*The Capitalist School in France*), who envisaged the school as a fragmented space composed of two distinctive formative pathways: the middle class (higher secondary education) and the proletarian (the primary vocational training)

The reception of Pierre Bourdieu et Jean-Claude Passeron's writings is however ambiguous as far as the teachers are concerned: although the majority agree with the denunciation of the role of cultural heritage and with the criticism of traditional teaching methods, they are however reluctant to admit to having a role in the imposition of the ideology of gift and the irreducibility of inequalities.

The works of the two sociologists have become the matrix of future reflections on the educational system. Although the popularisation of their theories makes them lose their complexity and appear simplistic, it broadens nonetheless, the impact of the debates on education.

The Sociology of Education After Pierre Bourdieu

Pierre Bourdieu's texts on education, particularly those co-authored with Jean-Claude Passeron, have inspired, since the 1970s, many sociological works testing the theory of reproduction. Numerous studies, often quantitative in nature, have, for instance, tried to measure scholastic democratisation. If Antoine Prost[57] stated in 1986 that an actual democratisation of secondary education took place between 1945 and 1960, other authors like Dominique Goux and Eric Maurin[58] have, on the contrary, highlighted the absence of evolution in the situation of scholastic inequalities between 1970 and 1993, despite the lengthening of the school curriculum and the increase in school enrolment. A study covering the entire period of the twentieth century, by Claude Thélot et Louis-André Vallet[59] showed that although the level of scholastic inequalities remains significant, social inequalities in schools have reduced.

Besides the studies seeking to measure social reproduction, new fields of research have opened up in the field of the sociology of education. Microsociological, qualitative and ethnographical research approaches have emerged that aim to better understand the leeway that actors have at their disposal in and around the school. The sociologists were, for instance, interested in the "paradoxical success" of students coming from social backgrounds that did not predispose them to scholastic success[60], the academic strategies put in place by the families, the students' educational experience[61], and they also ventured into the "black box" of the school by studying teaching effects, teacher effects and classroom effects on academic success[62]. New explanatory variables, other than economic and cultural levels, have been introduced into this framework such as, gender, migratory background, and whether attending a public or a private school.

2. THE QUESTION OF EDUCATIONAL DEMOCRATISATION (STÉPHANE BEAUD, 2002)

Stéphane Beaud is a sociologist and professor in the École normal supérieur de la rue d'Ulm. He worked extensively with the popular classes and the working classes, particularly in collaboration with Michel Pialoux. He also collaborated in *La Misère du monde* (*The Weight of the World*), published in 1993[63], under the direction of Pierre Bourdieu. In 2002, Stéphane Beaud published *80% au bac et après? Les enfants de la démocratisation scolaire*[64]. Fifteen years after launching the political slogan with the intention to bring in

80 per cent of a generation to high school, he revisited the effects of the massification of education at the upper-secondary school level and then at the university level.

The slogan "80% in high school" was first launched in 1985 by the French Minister of Education, Jean-Pierre Chevènement and then incorporated into Lionel Jospin's framework law governing education in 1989. At the time, the decision to improve the level of formal qualification of the French people was a result of the emergence of new technologies which required skilled workers. However, according to Stéphane Beaud, "under the pretext of the apparent democratisation of the education system, [its] only aim was to counter the problem of unemployment by keeping a growing proportion of the youth within the academic institution for an extended time" (p. 13). This slogan got support from parents belonging particularly to the lower classes, who till then, were under the impression that the school was not meant for their children. In the 1980s, the labour class was directly affected by the industrial restructuring, the deterioration of working conditions and mass unemployment, which especially affected the young graduates. Thus, for working class families, the school becomes "the place that delays the failure of their aspirations" (p. 10) The fundamental question that guides Stéphane Beaud's book is as follows: the policy of pursuing studies was it an "illusion or [a] genuine advancement" (p. 12) for children belonging to the lower classes?

The field survey carried out by Beaud focused primarily on children of migrant workers, who were the first in their families, thanks to the policy, to have access to high school education and eventually to a university education. For a period of ten years, from 1990 to 2000, Stéphane Beaud carried out an ethnological survey (observations, interviews, questionnaires) in the working class neighbourhood of

Gercourt, a city close to Montbéliard where the factories of Peugot are located. Stéphane Beaud defines his work as follows: "The purpose of the study involving high school students of the neighbourhood where I resided (Granvelle) was to analyse, from individual cases, how academic careers of children of labourers were built, one day at a time." (pp. 29-30) The book thus follows the different stages of education of the youth belonging to the Granvelle neighbourhood, right from secondary school to their entry into the workforce.

The difficulty, for the youth belonging to the lower classes, to fit into the scholastic culture, theorised by Pierre Bourdieu and Jean-Claude Passeron, appears to be the structuring characteristic on which the relationship between the youth of the working classes and the educational institution is built. Right from high school, students begin to notice the gap that exists between the culture of their neighbourhood and the culture in school: "unlike the other students from the working-class, these high-school students 'from the ghetto'—especially the boys—have a tendency to resist different initiatives, that focus on them, and are aimed at achieving educational integration. They completely refuse, for instance, to submit to the imposition of the method of refined reading practised in school and openly express their cultural 'reserve'. The culture that they are willing to defend, is the culture they know, it is the culture of their neighbourhood and that of their families, a culture disseminated by the media, the television, American cinema, etc." (p. 73). However, by manipulating the "weaknesses of the institution" (p. 14) resulting from the imposition of the policy of 80 per cent in high school (indulgent grading, flexibility in transition to the higher level, incorporation of specialised disciplines for weaker students) and by complying, at a minimum, to the expectations of the high school (participation in oral tests to compensate for deficiencies in writing skills, excellence in school work, refraining from cheating practices), the students of Granvelle manage to graduate from high school. The distance from the scholastic culture manifests itself once again at the time of choosing one's discipline after high school. The short courses (BTS, DUT), which are selective fields, close their doors to these students who clearly lack the social skills required to clear the interview (ability to move between language registers, modify physical appearances, the ability to "play along"). In other words, "that which constitutes a quality within the neighbourhood peer group —being oneself, taking pride in one's community and appearance, refusing to dress according to social norms— objectively transforms into a handicap and a factor working against his employability" (p. 140). As a result, the university, which is not selective, becomes their "back-up". Stéphane Beaud chose to exclusively follow the progress of four young people right from the beginning of their higher education: Nassim, Sabri, Djamel and Fehrat, who were representative of their generation of children coming from the lower classes and the first in their families to have access to higher education. These four students attended their first year of Deug, (equivalent to the first year of the graduate degree) in AES (Administration Économique et Sociale) in the university branch campus of Belfort, 20 kilometres from Gercourt. Despite the geographical proximity of the university and its relatively protective environment (fewer students, socially and academically homogeneous students, less demanding teachers), the university further worsens "the discrepancy between their abilities and the expectation of the institution" (p. 34).The geographical proximity to their homes has the adverse effect of low student participation in the structures conceived for them (library, university canteen, students' associations) and this distance from the academic institution goes hand in hand with a misunderstanding of the teaching methods which are different from those experienced in high school (autonomy, classes in lecture halls, less teacher supervision, non-mandatory attendance system, exams at the end of the teaching term, lower number of teaching hours). The non-appropriation of the academic vocabulary by the four "friends" is a sign of their failure to integrate into the institution: "Six months after the start of the school year, Nassim continues to say "cours marginaux" (marginal class) instead of "cours magistraux" (lecture class) when talking about the lectures [..]. The time spent as students in the university has in no way modified the way they speak" (pp. 162-163). The academic careers of the four boys finally end in the first year of Deug. While some choose to withdraw into their neighbourhoods as an escape route, others keep their hopes alive of working as officials in the public services. They are however withheld once again by the competitive examinations which they are unable to pass. The only avenues left for them are the precarious jobs of the public sector.

The evaluation of the social mobility of the career paths of the youth of Granvelle is thus ambiguous. If on one hand, the policy of "80% in high school" has enabled them to study and ultimately escape from the much despised factory work, the same policy has not, on the other hand, kept all its promises in terms of the hopes of social advancement that went largely unfulfilled. The massification of education was not accompanied by a genuine democratisation: new programmes for weaker students began to emerge, elimination was deferred and the teaching methods were not adapted to new students who were unable to adapt to the institution. Stéphane Beaud thus approved of the conclusion drawn by Pierre Bourdieu and Jean-Claude Passeron on the limitations of the massification of education.

NOTES

42. Durkheim, É., *L'Évolution pédagogique en France (1904-1905)* (1938), Paris, Presses Universitaires de France.
43. Bourdieu, P. et Passeron, J.-C., *Les Héritiers. Les étudiants et la culture* (1964), Paris, Minuit.
44. Bourdieu, P. et Passeron, J.-C., *La Reproduction. Éléments pour une théorie du système d'enseignement* (1970), Paris, Minuit.
45. *La Noblesse d'État. Grandes écoles et esprit de corps* (1980), Paris, Minuit.
46. Bernstein, B., *Educational Research* (1961), Vol. 3, pp. 163-176. Basil Bernstein a également écrit *Langage et classes sociales. Codes socio-linguistiques et contrôle social* (1975), Paris, Minuit.
47. The concept of the typical-ideal, as defined by Max Weber, refers to a sociological construction which presents itself as a model to better understand reality.
48. "L'école conservatrice. Les inégalités devant l'école et devant la culture", *Revue française de sociologie* (1966), Vol. 7, pp. 325-347, citation p. 336.
49. Boudon, R., *L'Idéologie ou l'origine des idées reçues* (1986), Paris, Fayard, p. 16.
50. Boudon, R., *L'Inégalité des chances. La mobilité sociale dans les sociétés industrielles* (1979 [1973]), Paris, Armand Colin.
51. Weber, M., *Économie et Société* (1971 [1921]), Paris, Plon, p. 285.
52. *La Domination masculine* (1998), Paris, Le Seuil.
53. "Stratégies de reproduction et modes de domination", *Actes de la Recherche en Sciences Sociales* (1994), Vol. 105, pp. 3-12.
54. "Classement, déclassement, reclassement", Actes de la Recherche en Sciences Sociales (1978), Vol. 24, pp. 2-22.
55. Prost, A., "Une sociologie stérile, la reproduction de Bourdieu et Passeron", *Esprit* (1970), pp. 851-861.
56. Baudelot, C., Establet, R., *L'École capitaliste en France* (1971), Paris, Maspéro.
57. *L'enseignement s'est-il démocratisé?* (1986), Paris, Presses Universitaires de France.
58. Goux, D., Maurin, E., "Origine sociale et destinée scolaire.

L'inégalité des chances devant l'enseignement à travers les enquêtes Formation-Qualification Professionnelle 1970, 1977, 1985 et 1993", *Revue française de sociologie* (1995), Vol. 36, pp. 81-121.

59. Thélot, C., Vallet, L.-A., "La réduction des inégalités sociales devant l'école depuis le début du siècle", *Économie et Statistique* (2000), No. 334, pp. 3-32.
60. Lahire, B., *Tableaux de familles. Heurs et malheurs scolaires en milieux populaires* (1995), Paris, Gallimard.
61. Dubet, F., Martuccelli, D., *À l'école : sociologie de l'expérience scolaire* (1996), Paris, Seuil.
62. Duru-Bellat, M., Van Zanten, A., *Sociologie de l'école* (2006), Paris, Armand Colin.
63. *La Misère du monde* (1993), Paris, Seuil.
64. Beaud, S., *80 % au bac... et après ? Les enfants de la démocratisation scolaire* (2002), Paris, La Découverte.

3

Sociology of Culture

Pierre Bourdieu's research on culture is anchored in the French tradition of conducting major investigations on the living conditions of the different social classes. Since the ground-breaking study of Frédéric Le Play (1806-1882) on *Les Ouvriers européens*[65] (*European Workers*), various research studies were carried out in order to better understand the connection between cultural practices and affiliation to a social class. On the basis of a survey on household budgets, Maurice Halbwachs in *La Classe ouvrière et les niveaux de vie*[66] (*The Working Class and Living Standards*), studied lifestyles and consumption patterns of manual workers, compared to that of office employees. After the Second World War, the finances, accommodation, work, family relations and even food consumption practices of manual labourers became the subject of a broader inquiry carried out by Paul-Henri Chombart de Lauwe.[67]

Pierre Bourdieu did not focus exclusively on the working class culture, he reflected in terms of "class cultures" by establishing a close relationship between cultural practices and social groups. By "culture", he meant the way people ate food, the way people set up their houses, how they dressed as well as their contact with works of art or with intellectual works (museum and theatre visits or reading practices, for instance). Both the meanings of the term "culture" are in fact intimately linked for Pierre Bourdieu.

According to him, "the dispositions which govern choices between the goods of legitimate culture cannot be fully understood unless they are reintegrated into the systems of dispositions, unless 'culture', in the restricted, normative sense of ordinary usage, is reinserted into 'culture' in the broad, anthropological sense and the elaborated taste for the more refined objects is brought back into relation with the elementary taste for the flavours of food."[68]

Pierre Bourdieu's consideration of "culture" is concomitant with a renewed political interest in the question of culture. In 1959, the Ministry of Cultural Affairs (presently the Ministry of Culture) was established and entrusted to André Malraux. His conception of culture was relatively restrictive as it only considered the high culture to be worthy of interest. For example, unlike classical music, traditional forms of folk music (music from Auvergne, Basque, Breton regions) were denied a place of importance within the framework of cultural policies. The obvious goal of the Ministry being the democratisation of high culture, i.e. making it accessible for everyone. The cultural policy which he intended to implement was based on sociological surveys. As a result, the Department for Studies and Research of the Ministry, headed by Augustin Girard, funded Pierre Bourdieu's survey of museum visitors in Europe in 1963. This study led to the publication of *L'Amour de l'art*[69] (*The Love of Art*) in 1969.

1. THE THEORY OF CULTURAL LEGITIMACY

Un Art moyen. Essai sur les usages sociaux de la photographie[70] (1965) (*Photography: A middle-brow art*), *L'Amour de l'art. Les musées d'art européens et leur public* (1969) (*The Love of Art. European Art Museums and Their Public*) and *La Distinction. Critique sociale du jugement* (1979) (*Distinction. A Social Critique of the Judgement of Taste*) are three major works where Pierre Bourdieu defines his sociology of culture. The first book, written in collaboration with Luc Boltanski, Robert Castel and Jean-Claude Chamboredon, was the result of a series of surveys, sponsored by Kodak-Pathé, on the different social uses of photography. The second book, written with Alain Darbel and Dominique Schnapper, is the outcome of a questionnaire-based survey on museum attendance, funded by the Department of Studies and Research. Both these books were the first to articulate the theory of cultural legitimacy that Pierre Bourdieu goes on to complete in *La Distinction* (1979). The latter, a critical book in the Bourdieusian body of works, is based on the research works mentioned above as well as on a new questionnaire-based survey which not only inquires into the reading practices and art preferences of individuals but even traces back the origin of their furniture and their clothes. Excerpts from interviews and portraits as well as photographs which give an account of the living conditions of the French people in the 1970s complete this methodological framework.

The theory developed in the three books, described as the "theory of cultural legitimacy", is based on the idea that cultural practices are not equal and that some practices are more indicative of their distinctiveness than others within the society, which means that by adopting these practices people rise in stature as they are in keeping with the practices of the higher classes.

1.1 Homology Between Social Hierarchy and Cultural Hierarchy

The Statistical Assessment: Classification of Cultural Practices Based on the Level of Education and Social Background

The first part of *L'Amour de l'art* (1969) aims at "taking into account all the factors that determine or encourage museum visits" (p. 35). The explanatory variables considered are gender, age, socio-professional category, income, level of education (certified by the diploma and practical knowledge of classical languages), the proximity of one's place of residence to the museum and opportunities to visit. The result of the assessment states that: museum attendance is directly proportional to the socio-professional category and the level of education; the latter however proves to be the most decisive factor. According to Pierre Bourdieu, "statistical results shows that access to cultural works is a privilege of the cultured classes" (p. 69) who, consequently, distinguish themselves from the middle and the lower classes. If social classes are classified based on the number of museum visits, they also distinguish themselves by the way they structure their visits. Based on his observation of the time dedicated to their visits by the respondents, Pierre Bourdieu highlighted an average of 22 minutes for the lower classes, 35 minutes for the middle classes and 47 minutes for the higher classes. Thus, different social classes do not have the same rapport with high culture.

Based on the analysis of diverse cultural practices (literature, cinema, music, paintings, leisure activities...), Pierre Bourdieu starts *La Distinction* (1979) by revealing statistical results that correspond to those presented in *L'Amour de l'art*. However these results are more generalised insofar as they apply to overall cultural behaviours and not particularly to those coming from high culture. He highlights a "very close relationship linking cultural practices (or the corresponding opinions) to educational capital (measured by qualifications) and, secondly, to social origin (measured by father's occupation)" (p. 12). Thus cultural practices of individuals vary according to their level of education and their social origins. He then goes on to establish the fact that "at equivalent levels of educational capital, the weight of social origin in the practice and preference-explaining system increases as one moves away from the most legitimate areas of culture" (p. 12). At equal levels of qualification, it is in the cultural domain, which is not subjected to academic learning, such as the cuisine, the interior decoration or furnishings, that the social origin becomes the most determining factor.

A Theory of the Social Classes

Pierre Bourdieu's sociology of culture is based on the theory of social classes. Unlike Karl Marx's analysis, this theory does not define social classes based solely on their position within the relations of production, that is, in terms of their economic strength (see Chapter 4). Social classes are defined, above all else, by taking into consideration their varied relationship with culture and more specifically with high culture.

Pierre Bourdieu studied the social classes that are constructed and not the classes existing in the real world. In his text entitled "Espace social et pouvoir symbolique"[71] (Social Space and Symbolic Power), Bourdieu emphasises this necessary differentiation: "My analysis especially in *La Distinction*, is misunderstood due to [..] the fact that the classes I talk about on paper are likely to be considered as real groups" (p. 153), that is, groups that are mobilised and work towards more visibility and recognition in society. Contrary to Karl Marx who infers the existence of a real class ("class in itself") based on his observation of the objective homogeneity of living conditions, Pierre Bourdieu maintains that the social classes he deals with are, first and foremost, "classes on paper", that is, classes in theory. From this perspective, the social classes fall under the explanatory classification developed by Bourdieu, which helps to anticipate their practices and attributes. In *La Distinction*,

Pierre Bourdieu endeavours to "construct [...] classes that are as homogeneous as possible" (p. 118) by referring to a plurality of indicators such as profession, level of education and economic strength.

According to Pierre Bourdieu, society is divided into three principal social groups: the bourgeoisie or the upper middle class, the middle class (or the "petty bourgeoisie") and the lower classes. Each of these groups is characterised by a specific "class culture", that corresponds to relatively homogeneous living conditions. There however exists partially defined subdivisions within these groups depending on the upward or downward trajectory of individuals who occupy the middle positions (see Chapter 4). The notion of trajectory presents a hierarchical conception of society that is oriented from the lower classes to the higher classes or, in Pierre Bourdieu's terms, from the dominated classes to the dominant classes. This social hierarchy is at the root of a hierarchy of cultural practices.

From Social Hierarchy to Cultural Hierarchy

According to Pierre Bourdieu, all cultural practices are not equal and some are more "legitimate" than others. The notion of "legitimacy" has been borrowed from Max Weber. It stands for the symbolic authority acquired by certain practices. In the text entitled "Comment être sportif"[72], Pierre Bourdieu countered games such as tennis, horse riding and golf—considered to be legitimate sports - with cycling, football and the pétanque, perceived as "ordinary" or "common". He particularly shows that unlike the *pétanque,* golf secures "profits of distinction" (p. 182) to those who practise it. The theory of cultural legitimacy is de facto founded on the idea that there exists a cultural hierarchy, that is, a classification of practices and disciplines that range from the least legitimate to the most legitimate.

The greater or lesser legitimacy of the cultural practices and disciplines is conferred by the value that the social classes, and notably the bourgeoisie, bestows upon it. Pierre Bourdieu is thus opposed to the idea that a cultural work has an intrinsic value: its value can only be social, that is attributed by the society and is therefore relative. More specifically, the upper classes, that correspond to the dominant classes, have the power to define these legitimate cultural works and practices. Again taking the example of sports, golf is practised more than the *pétanque* by members of the bourgeoisie as it is perceived as a legitimate sport. In this way, the dominant classes define "good" taste. Cultural legitimacy (identical to high culture) is nothing but the culture of the dominant classes. The same practice can thus become legitimate or illegitimate depending on the social position of the individuals who predominantly adopt it. In *La Distinction*, Pierre Bourdieu cites the example of *Le Beau Danube bleu* (*The Blue Danube*), a musical piece composed by Johann Strauss, to show how "a highbrow piece of music is devalued as a result of its popularisation" (p. 16). Its dissemination, and thus its popularisation among the dominated social classes, makes it illegitimate. Conversely, *Le Clavecin bien tempéré* (*The Well-Tempered Clavier*) by Jean-Sébastien Bach still preserves its legitimacy as it is a musical work essentially heard by members of the upper classes.

The hierarchy in cultural practices is thus rooted in social hierarchy: "The socially recognised hierarchy of the arts [..] corresponds to the social hierarchy of the consumers" (pp. I-II). Thus there exists a homology between social hierarchy and cultural hierarchy, that is, an overlapping of the social space and the space representing cultural practices. The cultural legitimacy of practices is determined by the social legitimacy of the people practising them. This is the reason why Pierre Bourdieu called his book on social uses of photography *Un Art moyen* (1965) (*A Middlebrow Art*): at that time, photography was still practised by the middle classes.

This *"homology between properties of agents and groups"* (*La Distinction*, p. 258) defines taste: "Choosing according to one's taste, means to identify the properties that are objectively granted to his position and are harmonised amongst them" (p. 258). Pierre Bourdieu thus distinguishes between "three types of tastes that basically correspond to education levels and social classes" (p. 14): legitimate taste, or the taste for legitimate works of art (for example *The Well-Tempered Clavier*, the painters Pieter Bruegel and Francisco de Goya); "middlebrow" taste brings together lesser-known works of the major arts (the musical piece *Rhapsody in Blue* by George Gershwin, the painters Maurice Utrillo, Bernard Buffet and Auguste Renoir) and famous works of the minor arts (the singers Jacques Brel and Gilbert Bécaud); "popular" taste "represented here by the choice of works identified as 'light music' or classical music devalued by their popularisation, as in the case of *The Blue Danube* [..] and especially songs totally devoid of artistic ambition or pretension such as Luis Mariano, Guétary or Petula Clark" (p. 16)

1.2 Habitus as the Principle that Generates Cultural Practices

Taste, a Social Construct

According to the philosopher Emmanuel Kant, beauty is what is universally pleasurable. It is the object of a disinterested satisfaction (which distinguishes it from the 'agreeable') and it can be defined as "purposive without purpose" or a "final without end", that is, an end in itself with no particular purpose. In *La Distinction* (1979), Pierre Bourdieu refutes the idea which states that the ability to appreciate art is universal and innate. He shows, with the help of statistical data and interviews, that beauty is not defined in the same way by everyone and that only the most qualified social groups share the Kantian idea of beauty. The least educated have a different conception of beauty. For them, beauty is more contextual than universal (for example, when they are shown an image they say: "It's fine, if it's meant to be shown to children" or "it's not bad for a photo-report"). They are more interested in the functionality of the works (utility, authorisation, moral character, informative dimension) rather than in their formal qualities. The difference in the criteria of aesthetic judgement mobilised in accordance with the cultural capital of individuals is clearly manifest in the following example. When Pierre Bourdieu showed the picture of the hands of an old woman to different people, the least qualified had a relatively simple interpretation. Rather than making a purely aesthetic judgement of the object, they empathised with the subject. Take for instance, the reaction of a Parisian factory worker: "Well I never! Her hands are extremely deformed [..] This old lady must have worked really hard". The reactions become more and more abstract as we move up the social ladder. People from the upper classes attribute a symbolic and non-specific value to things that are represented. Making references to other forms of art (painting, sculpture, literature), linking photography to larger categories, is also very frequent. Thus, an engineer in Paris makes the following observation of the photograph: "I think that it's a very beautiful photo. It symbolises the world of labour. It reminds me of the old servant described by Flaubert." (*La Distinction*, p. 46) The ability to appreciate art as an end in itself, according to the Kantian perspective, implies the possession of cognitive tools for deciphering and decoding the artistic language, which means, a form of "cultural competence" which is not immediately accessible to everyone.

Family and School, Places to Learn Cultural Competence

Paradoxically, while art is taught very little in school, it is the academic capital that is best able to recognise the inequalities in the appreciation of works of culture. This means that aesthetic competence is not only acquired through learning in terms of the content (authors, genres, schools and movements) but it is also a fruit of a "scholarly disposition", artistic or otherwise, that the school transmits through education. Thus the school provides analytical tools, in literature for instance, that can subsequently be transposed to other disciplines. According to Pierre Bourdieu, the need for culture, created by the school (which simultaneously also gives the means to satisfy the need), becomes all the more important for the more cultured. This explains the disparity in museum attendance based on qualification: "The 'cultural need' intensifies as it is satisfied [and] the absence of practice is accompanied by the absence of the feeling of its absence" (*L'Amour de l'art*, p. 69). Thus, initial educational inequalities transform into post facto cumulative cultural inequalities.

However the school is not the only institution transmitting cultural competence. The family also plays a major role. Individuals who apply their legitimate taste with great ease are not only the most qualified but also come from a cultured background. The school validates, to a certain extent, the culture acquired in the family (see Chapter 2). Thus "the dominant definition of the legitimate way of appropriating culture and works of art favours those who have had early access to legitimate culture, in a cultured household, outside of scholastic disciplines, since even within the educational system it devalues scholarly knowledge and interpretation as 'scholastic' or even 'pedantic' in favour of direct experience and simple delight." (*La Distinction*, p. II). Within the family, cultural competence ('good taste') is unconsciously acquired since a very young age, even before partaking in discussions, through an immersion in a cultured environment at an early stage. The experience of making choices that either arouse approval or mockery, teaches individuals to unconsciously act in such a way that their practices and tastes are validated by their surroundings. The acquisition of cultural competence by an individual is thus dependent on the objective probabilities of his ability to validate it around himself. As a result of this imperceptible familiarisation with a cultural competence within the family, people fail to recognise the acquired nature of "good taste" and consider it to be a "natural taste", that is spontaneous. Thus aesthetic experience can be felt freely and subjectively even though it is, according to Pierre Bourdieu, nothing by the internalisation of a cultural arbitrary.

Habitus and Lifestyle

In Bourdieu's opinion, all cultural choices, besides the choices made in the field of the arts, are an expression of the class habitus (see Chapter 1). The different living conditions of the social classes produce different habitus that are unique. Habitus is defined as a "principle which generates and organises practices and representations."[73] This means that the habitus is not only the origin of tastes and practices (especially in the cultural sphere), but it also establishes a relationship and coherence between practices. In this way, it encourages the emergence of a "lifestyle" that is constituted by common cultural choices made by a social class in different areas (type of food, language, taste for music and the visual arts, choice of decor, clothing and sports...). The example of the old cabinet maker in *La Distinction* (1979) further illustrates this aspect: "An old cabinet maker's world view, the way he manages his budget, his time or his body, his use of language and choice of clothing are fully present in his ethic of scrupulous, impeccable craftsmanship and in the aesthetic of work for work's sake which leads him to measure the beauty of his products by the care and patience that have gone into them." (pp. 193-194).

Habitus encourages the same type of attitude in different domains. The opposition, highlighted by Pierre Bourdieu, between the lower classes who emphasise strength, quantity, substance and the middle classes who give importance to form, to lightness and to distance, is prevalent in matters of food as well as the choice of sports activities. Bourdieu shows that in the realm of food, "the working classes are more attentive to the strength of the (male) body than its shape, and tend to go for products that are both cheap and nutritious, those practising liberal professions prefer products that are tasty, healthy, light and not fattening." (*La Distinction*, p. 210) Similarly in the field of sports, the working classes have a functional relationship with the body that makes them choose sports "that require a greater investment of effort, and sometimes even cause hurt and pain (like boxing), and bodily harm, like motorcycle races."[74] On the other hand, the middle classes prefer activities with limited corporal involvement and deferred benefits (slower ageing, better health). They turn to golf, horse riding, fencing or race walking which avoid direct contact with the opponent and maintains a distance between them. The image of the body is linked to the worldview, that is distinct for every social class, and helps to understand the tastes and preferences of each social class in diverse realms and practices.

1.3 Taste, Between Imitation and Distinction

Taste as an Imitation of the Dominant Taste

The three principal social classes (the bourgeoisie, the petty-bourgeoisie and the popular class) defined by Bourdieusian sociology are characterised by their special relationship with culture. As the uppermost class in the social hierarchy, the bourgeoisie is considered to be the dominant class. Its position empowers it to define legitimate taste, in other words, the taste that serves as a point of reference for the entire society. Although this taste refers to a specific taste that is socially constructed through socialisation within the family and in school, it is considered to be a "natural" taste. This situation represents a symbolic violence that imposes a cultural arbitrary (validation of high art, optimal ease and distance) on the other social classes. The "ideology of natural taste" promoted by the dominant class in the cultural domain is identical to the "ideology of gift" in the academic domain (see Chapter 2). However the dominant class is not completely united when it comes to the definition of legitimate taste: it is subdivided into fractions of classes who are embroiled in symbolic conflicts, in a bid to define good taste. On the one hand, the most cultured dominant class (professors, journalists...) defend a concept of culture that Pierre Bourdieu calls the "ascetic aristocratism". They promote traditional elitist cultural practices (listening to classical music, visiting museums, reading classical literature) that demand self-discipline and distance. The rich dominant class (commerce and industry heads, liberal professions) adopt a hedonistic morality when it comes to consumption and cultural practices. While still remaining elitist (travelling, purchasing works of art), they are more inclined towards the world of luxury.

The high culture promoted by the bourgeoisie serves as

a point of reference for the petty-bourgeoisie, which means, members of the middle classes. The latter are characterised by their willingness to attain an upward social mobility that makes them adhere, without reservation, to the dominant culture. Pierre Bourdieu describes their attitude as a "cultural good will". Cultural good will manifests itself in deference to the legitimate culture and as a desire for self-cultivation. The petty-bourgeoisie or the middle classes tend to emulate the way of life led by the dominant classes. They strive to adopt alternative practices, which, although show all external signs of legitimate culture, are more accessible to them. For instance, photography is practised as an alternative to painting. They are also interested in other minor art forms: preferring the operetta to the opera. All such efforts to immerse oneself into legitimate culture are nevertheless tainted by the recurrence of instances of lack of taste which reveal the absence of familiarity with the dominant culture. Linguistic hypercorrection, for example, is proof of the inability of the working classes to completely adapt to the codes of the dominant culture. Just like the dominant class, the middle class is heterogeneous. It is divided into three fractions, based on the social trajectories of the individuals who make up these groups. Each fraction is defined by its own lifestyle. The declining traditional middle class is made up of artisans and traders who have traditional, austere tastes. They give great importance to rigour and work ethics. They are opposed to the growing middle class of executives, which comprises salaried employees, mid-manager level employees, primary school teachers and skilled workers... who subordinate everything to the idea of social elevation. Their customs and practices can thus be distinguished by their discipline and seriousness. Finally, the new petty bourgeoisie comprises, on the one hand, of people of the bourgeoisie (*déclassé*), who lose their class position for not having the necessary educational qualifications and on the other hand, of members of the petty bourgeoisie who have a strong cultural capital, but lack the social capital required to integrate into the bourgeoisie. The new petty bourgeoisie work mainly in the artistic field and in the fields of consulting or communication which strive to gain social recognition. These individuals look for accoutrements of culture, by buying popular science journals for instance, and by improving their linguistic skills. The middle class, comprising of people on an upward trajectory as well as on a declining trajectory, is thus characterised by the most heterogeneous consumption practices as compared to the higher and the popular classes.

The popular class, likened to the working class, is, according to Pierre Bourdieu, the most homogeneous of social classes. Its relationship with culture is characterised by its "choice of the necessary". The limited economic means of the working class forces it to restrict itself to a simple life and to opt for the practical and the functional rather than the aesthetic. They however do not consider it to be a constraint but rather as a "choice", a genuine taste for simplicity.

According to Pierre Bourdieu, popular taste does not have a positive existence: it is but a downgrading of the dominant taste. It is limited to "scattered fragments of a more or less traditional high culture [..] that are selected and reinterpreted depending on the fundamental principles of the class habitus and eventually integrated into their unified world view" (*La Distinction*, p. 459). Due to the absence of autonomy, popular taste is incapable of asserting itself as a counter-culture that is likely to question the legitimacy of the dominant culture.

This conception of popular culture as a heteronomous culture (i.e. its principles are defined externally) was questioned by Claude Grignon and Jean-Claude Passeron in *Le Savant et le Populaire*[75] (*The Erudite and the Popular*). In their opinion, there exists two antagonistic ways to consider popular culture in sociology that are, both, equally open to criticism. The first approach is to consider popular culture as "a significant autonomous universe" by ignoring the symbolic effects of economic and social domination that weighs upon the popular classes. According to the authors, this perspective is laden with "populism", insofar as the underlying cultural relativism leads to the conclusion that popular culture is more authentic and morally superior than high culture. The second approach, articulated by Pierre Bourdieu, consists of opposing the first approach and to consider popular culture solely from the viewpoint of its "symbolic dependence" on high culture, by refusing to see what, in popular culture, is unique and relatively autonomous. This perspective is defined as a "miserabilist" approach as it considers popular cultures to be impoverished. The theory of legitimate culture which is well suited to study high culture, seems thus to be less relevant for describing popular culture.

Distinction at the Heart of the Social Game

In the Bourdieusian theory of culture, the first mechanism that explains the hierarchy of tastes is that of imitation: each social class tends to imitate the taste of the superior class but achieve only a degraded form of that taste. Furthermore, the practice of imitation is harmful for the classes whose culture is imitated, in as much as it makes them lose their exclusivity and they are exposed to the risk of losing their dominant position. A second mechanism, that of distinction, is put into effect by the higher classes, in order to maintain a distance from the other classes.

Distinction, which is also the title of the pioneering work

of Pierre Bourdieu, must be understood in two different ways; firstly, as the property of the "distinguished" classes and secondly, as the process that leads to the acquisition of this property by maintaining a distance from the other social classes. Thus by "distinction", Pierre Bourdieu means a "rank to be upheld"and a "distance to be maintained" (*La Distinction*, p. 61). The desire for distinction of the dominant classes was highlighted ever since the end of the nineteenth century by the American sociologist Thorstein Veblen in *La Théorie de la classe de loisir*[76] (*The Theory of the Leisure Class*). In this book, the author demonstrates that the "leisure class", i.e. the class of people who are wealthy enough to choose not to work, find ways to set themselves apart from the other social classes and establish their superiority by the (demonstrated) conspicuous consumption of specific material goods. Thus the women wear corsets, flowing skirts and high heels that prevent them from doing any kind of work, indicating their membership of the leisure class. The inclination to imitate these practices by the lower social classes forces the upper classes to evade and switch to consumption of new products. However according to Pierre Bourdieu, distinction is not a matter of expenditure alone, since it relies essentially on cultural practices and aesthetic preferences. Moreover, since distinction is an unconscious expression of habitus, it is not necessarily sought-after intentionally. Nonetheless, the headlong rush by the upper classes is an evasive mechanism that is constantly at play. According to Pierre Bourdieu, as soon as a practice becomes popular, it loses its distinctive feature since it is "downgraded by dissemination" (*La Distinction*, p. 16). This disseminated practice is thus abandoned by the dominant classes who turn (temporarily) towards other exclusive, and therefore, more distinctive practices. This explains why, for instance, towards the end of the 1990s, the appropriation of the brand Lacoste by the youth of the working classes, which till then was a prerogative of the upper classes, resulted in a sharp decline in the distinctive value of the brand. The upper classes subsequently turned towards other brands that were more exclusive and less circulated.

According to Pierre Bourdieu, "tastes are undoubtedly first and foremost distastes, disgust provoked by horror or visceral intolerance ('nauseating') of the tastes of others" (*La Distinction*, p. 60). While each social class tries to imitate the taste of the classes superior to them, they simultaneously tend to also distinguish themselves from the classes that are inferior to them. Thus, the dominant classes establish their cultural choices in the fields of art, furnishings, table manners, clothing etiquette...like so many other aesthetic decisions which disagree with the choices made by the middle and the popular classes. The middle class or the petty bourgeoisie follow the same trend with respect to the popular classes who are considered to be "repulsive" for all the others. The employees of the middle-management, for instance, refuse to take realistic photographs, such as family photographs, in order to distinguish themselves from the practices of the popular classes (*Un Art moyen*, 1965). On the contrary, middle managers aim to get closer to the centre of legitimate culture by giving to photography the dignity of an art form. This aversion to the taste of inferior social groups takes place even within a social class, between the old and the new fractions. The old fractions of the bourgeoisie, for example, express their distaste for the new bourgeoisie who are considered to be too "pedantic" in their expression of legitimate taste.

Regardless, taste is generally a unifying force for members of a class. From this perspective, Edmond Goblot showed in 1925, in *La Barrière et le Niveau*[77] (*The Barrier and the Level*), that taste was a means to blend into a class and also a means to keep a distance from people of other classes. Like Pierre Bourdieu, Goblot observes that the bourgeoisie does not distinguish itself as much through its wealth, as it does through its practices. In fact, cultural practices make it possible to compensate for the absence of legal barriers between the bourgeoisie and the lower classes. Through their lifestyle, the bourgeois blend into their class (level) and distinguish themselves from the lower classes (barrier): "Do the same as everyone else! That is the level. Do not be common! That is a barrier." (p. 66) As far as clothing is concerned, wearing a suit in the nineteenth century associated people with the bourgeoisie, since all the bourgeois wore suits and it distinguished them from all the people who did not wear suits. Although Pierre Bourdieu does not explicitly mention Edmond Goblot in *La Distinction*, their conclusions seem to be in agreement.

Taste for Pierre Bourdieu does not exist relationally since it always appears to be a quest for imitation or for distinction. This conception calls into question some popular sayings that suppose a naturalness and a purely subjective taste when stating that "to each his/her own taste".

2. LEGITIMISATION OF A CULTURAL PRACTICE: EXAMPLE OF JAZZ (Jean-Louis Fabiani, 1986)

"Choices always owe a share of their worth to the value of the person who makes those choices." (*Distinction*, p. 100) According to the Bourdieusian theory of culture, the legitimacy of a cultural practice stems from the social legitimacy of the people who practise it. Since the dominant classes determine dominant taste, they have the power to consecrate, i.e. legitimise, practices that were not considered to be legitimate earlier, since they were practised by the popular classes.

In "Carrières improvisées: Théories et pratiques de la

musique de jazz en France[78]" ("Improvised Carriers: Theories and Practices of Jazz Music in France"), Jean-Louis Fabiani, who is the academic director in the École des hautes études en sciences sociales (The School for Advanced Studies in the Social Sciences), studies the social process which enabled jazz to transition from the status of an "outcast art form" (p. 242) to that of a legitimate art form in France. This process involves various agencies of legitimisation which are closer to dominant cultural centres: academic critics, a cultured public and cultural institutions representing legitimate culture.

The Process of Legitimisation of Jazz in France

According to Jean-Louis Fabiani, firstly critical studies produced in universities enabled jazz to transition from the status of "black music" to that of "middlebrow art". In fact, these academic critics, who are closer to legitimate culture, have an aesthetic and scholarly relationship with art which enables them to (re)define this music. This work helps to "create a belief in the existence of this musical form" (p. 235) and to "demonstrate that jazz, like any serious music, is likely to be the subject of scholarly history" (p. 239).

The legitimisation of jazz is also the result of the emergence of a community of jazz lovers. The jazz audience, in France, is composed of fractions of intellectuals of the dominant classes who try to distinguish themselves from legitimate culture while, at the same time, refraining from making popular choices, and from the petty-bourgeois who see this musical form as a substitute for practices that are more legitimate, but are inaccessible to them due to the lack of necessary cultural resources.

These movements combined lead to the transformation of jazz, its practices and the contexts of its reception. Jazz gradually moves away from its former "purely functional forms" (accompanying music, dance music, or recreational music) and becomes an end in itself, just like the legitimate art forms. Jazz is increasingly being heard in established places (concert halls, museums) and the audience's attitude is more civilised: although they still keep the rhythm with their foot or the hand, they do it in silence. The redefinition of jazz is however not uniform. If, on the one hand, there appears a jazz that has the "discipline of serious music" (paying attention to form, shift towards a written form of jazz), on the other hand, there are jazz musicians who remain "playfully spontaneous" which is characteristic of its initial expressions. This duality conveys the ambiguity that surrounds jazz with respect to legitimate musical forms and it leads Jean-Louis Fabiani to define jazz as a "false-legitimate" musical form (p. 238).

This musical form gets institutional recognition in the 1980s. In 1981, jazz musicians got financial aide, which was earlier reserved for serious music, for the promotion of their music. Thereafter, the Orchestre National du Jazz (National Jazz Orchestra) was created. According to Jean-Louis Fabiani, "for the purpose of cultural administration, in the name of a policy of broadening the cultural legacy by including all forms of expression, musical forms were de-prioritised and an authentic jazz studies programme was created in conservatories" (p. 242). Jazz thus became "a sort of a double of serious music" (p. 243).

Other Cultural Practices on the Road to Legitimisation

Just like Jean-Louis Fabiani, a number of sociologists were interested in the process of the legitimisation of popular cultural practices based on the perspective established by Pierre Bourdieu. This is the case especially of Luc Boltanski,[79] who studied the legitimisation of comic books by a cultured public, and that of Sylvia Faure and Marie-

Carmen Garcia[80] who worked on the changing social value of hip-hop.

3. THE THEORY OF CULTURAL LEGITIMACY IN QUESTION

Due to its explanatory quality, the Bourdieusian theory of cultural legitimacy comes across today as a genuine model that enables cultural sociologists to position themselves either by validating, by modifying or by contradicting it.

3.1 Eclecticism of Cultural Practices
(Richard Peterson and Roger Kern, 1996)

The Bourdieusian theory of cultural legitimacy found some support in the United States with the emergence of a number of studies, especially after the English translation of *La Distinction* in 1984. In an article entitled "Social Class and Arts Consumption: The Origins and Consequences of Class Differences in Exposure to the Arts in America" (1978[81]), Paul DiMaggio and Michael Useem corroborated the vital importance of the level of education for gaining access to high culture in the American society. In 1992, Richard Peterson and Peter Simkus published "How Musical Tastes Mark Occupational Status Group,"[82] in which, with the help of quantitative data taken in 1982, the authors showed that the upper classes were characterised not only by their proximity to cultivated musical genres, such as the opera or classical music, but also as a result of their eclectic musical preferences. In addition to cultivated music, many people of the upper classes also enjoyed listening to popular genres of music. The data from 1982 is revisited and compared with new data of 1992 by Richard Peterson, professor of sociology of the Vanderbilt University of Nashville, and his student Roger Kern in 1996. Their article "Changing Highbrow Taste: From Snob to Omnivore,"[83] a product of this comparative study, highlights the increasing eclecticism in musical tastes among the upper classes.

Increasing Eclecticism in Musical Tastes: From Snob to Omnivore

In the quantitative analysis, Richard Peterson and Roger Kern distinguish between two categories of connoisseurs of classical music and of opera: the snobs and the omnivores. The first category is limited to legitimate musical preferences while the second set of people are open to lesser legitimate musical genres (*"lowbrow"* or *"middlebrow"*, i.e. "downmarket" or "less intellectual"). By comparing the data from 1992 to that from 1982, the authors discovered that the number of omnivores have increased among the elites and there were very few snobs remaining amongst them. The upper classes are thus increasingly characterised by their eclectic tastes in music, while the popular classes are mainly composed of "univores" who have exclusive musical interests among the *"lowbrow"* genres. Based on the statistical regression model, the authors focus on the generational effect (the replacement of generational cohorts) and the period effect (change in cultural preferences in the 1980s) to explain the increase in eclecticism amongst the upper classes.

Questioning the Theory of Cultural Legitimacy?

The increasing eclecticism in cultural practices puts an end to the strict homology between social hierarchy and cultural hierarchy which was the foundation of the theory of cultural legitimacy. The upper classes' taste for legitimate genres is not accompanied by a dislike for the lesser legitimate genres.

Although they complicate the modality of articulation between social segmentation and cultural practices, the results drawn by Richard Peterson and Roger Kern nevertheless, do not question the existence of symbolic boundaries between social classes. From this perspective, while referring to the works of Pierre Bourdieu they write: "omnivorism does not imply an indifference to distinctions. Its emergence is rather the formulation of new rules that govern the symbolic boundaries."[84] Eclecticism thus becomes the new strategy for distinguishing between dominant classes.

In order to fulfil this function, eclecticism must not be practised in a vague manner. What matters in the case of distinction is not so much the object consumed but the manner in which it is consumed. Hence the omnivores do not understand country music in the same way as the fans of country music who completely identify with it: they intellectualise and aestheticise this music just as they do for jazz, blues and rock. Despite the openness of the upper classes towards these forms of music, the manner in which *"lowbrow"* or *"middlebrow"* genres are enjoyed remains nevertheless differentiated depending on the social background.

Following the works of Richard Peterson, the French sociologists highlighted the same eclectic phenomenon in the musical tastes (Philippe Coulangeon[85]) and in the cultural practices of the French upper classes (Olivier Donnat[86]). They concluded that there is a complexification rather than a questioning of the theory of cultural legitimacy.

3.2 Dissonant Cultural Practices and Preferences
(Bernard Lahire, 2004)

A professor of sociology in the École normale supérieure in Lyon, Bernard Lahire's research areas include culture, the school and the family. His research leads to the discussion of Pierre Bourdieu's works, who was also his professor. In 2004, in his book *La Culture des individus. Dissonances culturelles et distinction de soi,*[87] Lahire revisits the theory of cultural legitimacy and develops his theory which states that "the boundary between 'cultural legitimacy' and 'cultural illegitimacy' does not only separate different social groups or classes [..] [but]—an important fact that is never raised—also divides the different cultural practices and preferences of individuals within the same group and across all classes." (p. 30).

Cultural Dissonances

Bernard Lahire suggests "changing the perspective" (p. 10) with respect to Pierre Bourdieu's sociology of culture by first focusing on the differences in the levels of legitimacy of cultural practices of each individual ("intra-individual variations") before looking at the differences in the cultural practices among social classes ("inter-individual variations"). He cites the example of the philosopher Ludwig Wittgenstein who openly declared—contrary to expectations—loving detective novels and westerns, in other words, objects that were less legitimate, in order to highlight the existence of dissonant individual profiles characterised by strong intra-individual variations. He reproached Bourdieu for not paying attention to these "cultural dissonances" that can challenge the idea of coherent tastes and lifestyles.

With the help of a statistical study, Bernard Lahire kept an account of individuals with dissonant cultural profiles, within his sample. For example, dissonant profiles were recorded that ranged from individuals who liked the most legitimate literature to those who listened to French popular music. Bernard Lahire discovered that these profiles are statistically very common even though they are found mostly among the middle and the upper classes and not so much among the popular classes. The individual is thus most often divided between a "legitimate self" and an "illegitimate self". The rare consonant profiles "occupy completely opposite positions in the social space" (p. 23); they are characterised either by cultural deprivation, or by their adherence to the most legitimate cultural frameworks

From Habitus to a Plurality of Dispositions and Cultural Contexts

The cultural dissonances brought to light in *La Culture des individus* dismisses the possibility of a coherent habitus that acts as "principle which generates and organises all practices." In order to take stock of the intra-individual variations in cultural behaviour, Bernard Lahire focused on a variety of socialising experiences—through the family, but also the school, professional situation, conjugal situation, etc.—which allow an individual to incorporate a plurality of dispositions and cultural skills. In a previous book in 1998, *L'Homme pluriel. Les ressorts de l'action,*[88] Lahire defends the idea that each individual has not one but multiple habitus, that he acquires in diverse situations of socialisation. These internalised dispositions and skills are either put on standby or are activated depending on the cultural context. Bernard Lahire thus concludes that "on the one hand, the plurality of dispositions and skills and on the other hand, the different contexts of their realisation can sociologically explain the variety of behaviours of the same individual" (*La Culture des individus,* p. 14).

Questioning the Theory of Cultural Legitimacy?

Bernard Lahire does not challenge the theory of legitimacy as much as he improves upon it through the assessment of the inherent tensions of the habitus. He thus retains the idea of a cultural hierarchy of practices, that is established not only from the social hierarchy but also "by taking into account the internal properties of an activity" (p. 99) like for instance, its collective or individual character. He thus categorically dismisses cultural relativism, according to which, henceforth, "everything is valid" (p. 85).

From the interviews that he conducted, Bernard Lahire shows that individuals with dissonant cultural profiles are conscious of the internal hierarchy of their more or less legitimate practices. He "reveals the different levels of commitment and, in this case, of self-withdrawal vis-a-vis the cultural practices that are perceived to be less legitimate" (p. 54). According to the respondents, a television series such as *Sous le soleil or* a reality show like *Loft Story* can be watched not for the merit of its content but due to curiosity, for laughs (figuratively) or as entertainment. People are clear about their practices. They express their symbolic struggles through their cultural investments.

3.3 Radical Critics of the Theory of Cultural Legitimacy

The most radical critics of the theory of cultural legitimacy dismiss the idea of cultural hierarchy that neither Richard Peterson nor Bernard Lahire had questioned. Many sociologists assume that there is a loss in the coherence of high culture, i.e. all the practices and preferences considered to be "legitimate" in the 1960s. While the elements of high culture do not seem to immediately characterise the upper classes, Olivier Donnat (2004) asks a vital question: "Who can today [...] claim that they do not feel a certain predicament when they have to [..] spell out the contents of [high culture]?" (p. 94)

Certain sociologists such as Hervé Glevarec,[89] refuse to categorise cultural practices based on a hierarchical order by stating that the degree of legitimacy attributed to them is only a proof of the arbitrariness of the sociologist. Others, like Antoine Hennion,[90] propose a sociology of taste which is disconnected from the concerns of the theory of cultural legitimacy, and focus on the relation between the individual and the object, and on the supporting mediations that help to express the development of taste.

NOTES

65. Le Play, F., *Les Ouvriers européens* (1971, [1855]), Paris, Hachette.
66. Halbwachs, M., *La Classe ouvrière et les niveaux de vie* (1970, [1913]), Paris, Archives contemporaines.
67. Chombart de Lauwe, P.-H., *La Vie quotidienne des familles ouvrières* (1956), Paris, CNRS.
68. *La Distinction. Critique sociale du jugement* (1979), Paris, Minuit, p. 109.
69. Bourdieu, P. et Darbel, A., *L'Amour de l'art. Les musées d'art européens et leur public* (1969), Paris, Minuit.
70. Bourdieu, P. (dir.), *Un Art moyen. Essai sur les usages sociaux de la photographie* (1965), Paris, Minuit.
71. "Espace social et pouvoir symbolique", in *Choses dites* (1987), Paris, Minuit, pp. 147-166.
72. "Comment être sportif?", in *Questions de sociologie*, Paris, Minuit, pp. 173-195.
73. *Le Sens pratique* (1980), Paris, Minuit, p. 88.
74. *Questions de sociologie* (1984), Paris, Minuit, pp. 192-193.
75. Grignon, C., Passeron, J.-C., *Le Savant et le Populaire. Misérabilisme et populisme en sociologie et en littérature* (1989), Paris, Gallimard.
76. Veblen, T., *La Théorie de la classe de loisir* (1970, [1899]), Paris, Gallimard.
77. Goblot, E., *La Barrière et le Niveau* (1925), Paris, Presse Universitaires de France.
78. Fabiani, J.-L., "Carrières improvisées : théories et pratiques de la musique de jazz en France", *Sociologie de l'art* (1986), Paris, L'Harmattan, pp. 231-245.
79. Boltanski, L., "La constitution du champ de la bande dessinée", *Actes de la Recherche en Sciences Sociales* (1975), Vol. 1, pp. 37-59.
80. Faure, S., Garcia, M.-C., *Culture hip-hop, jeunes des cités et politiques publiques* (2005), Paris, La Dispute.
81. DiMaggio, P. et Useem, M., "Social Class and Arts

Consumption: The Origins and Consequences of Class Differences in Exposure to the Arts in America", *Theory and Society* (1978), Vol. 5, No. 2, pp. 141-161.

82. Peterson, R. et Simkus, P., (1992). "How Musical Tastes Mark Occupational Status Groups", in M. Lamont et M. Fournier (dir.), *Cultivating Differences,* Chicago, University of Chicago Press, pp. 152-168.
83. Peterson, R. et Kern, R., "Changing Highbrow Taste: From Snob to Omnivore", *American Sociological Review* (1996), Vol. 61, No. 5, pp. 900-907.
84. "Omnivorousness does not imply an indifference to distinctions. Rather its emergence may suggest the formulation of new rules governing symbolic boundaries", p. 904.
85. Coulangeon, P., "La stratification sociale des goûts musicaux. Le modèle de la légitimité culturelle en question", *Revue française de sociologie* (2003), Vol. 44, pp. 3-33.
86. Donnat, O., "Les univers culturels des Français", *Sociologie et Sociétés* (2004), Vol. 36, No. 1, pp. 87-103.
87. Lahire, B., *La Culture des individus. Dissonances culturelles et distinction de soi* (2004), Paris, La Découverte.
88. Lahire, B., *L'Homme pluriel. Les ressorts de l'action* (1998), Paris, Nathan.
89. Glevarec, H., "La fin du modèle classique de la légitimité culturelle. Hétérogénéisation des ordres de légitimité et régime contemporain de justice culturelle. L'exemple du champ musical", in E. Maigret et E. Macé (dir.), *Penser les médiacultures. Nouvelles pratiques et nouvelles approches de la représentation du monde* (2005), Paris, Colin/INA, pp. 69-102.
90. Hennion, A., *La Passion musicale. Une sociologie de la médiation* (1993), Paris, Métailié.

4

The Theory of Social Space

In his writings, especially the most recent among them, Pierre Bourdieu theorises the notion of "social space" and introduces a new way to understand society. Social space is structured according to the social distances that separate the agents. Individuals are placed within this space depending on their greater or lesser worth in "capital". Since everyone vies for dominant positions, the social space seems to be a space of struggle. These struggles focus on specific issues within the framework of what Pierre Bourdieu calls "fields".

1. CAPITAL AND SOCIAL SPACE

Pierre Bourdieu borrows the economic term "capital" from Karl Marx, that allowed him to highlight the positioning of individuals in relation to each other within the social space.

1.1 Capital at the Foundation of a Multidimensional Social Space

Definition of Capital

In Karl Marx's theory, individuals are defined as either bourgeois or proletarian based on whether or not they possess economic capital. The owners of the means of production are opposed to the latter who only possess labour power. The notion of capital is thus limited to only the means of production. Pierre Bourdieu does not restrict capital to the economic sphere alone. He envisages the existence of different kinds of capital (economic capital, cultural capital, social capital, symbolic capital, political capital...) which emerge as social resources for the agents. Perceived as a stock with a more or less significant volume, each type of capital is the fruit of an accumulation with the objective of obtaining a profit or a return, material or not.

The Bourdieusian analysis distinguishes four principal types of capital: economic capital, cultural capital, social capital and symbolic capital. These capitals are defined in the following way:

- **Economic Capital**
  Economic capital means all the economic resources of an individual, his material heritage as well as his income. Having economic capital allows an individual to easily acquire other types of capital.
- **Cultural Capital**
  Cultural capital corresponds to cultural resources that allow an individual to appreciate the assets and practices of high culture. The notion of "cultural capital " was introduced by Pierre Bourdieu and Jean-Claude Passeron in *La Reproduction. Éléments pour une théorie du système d'enseignement.*[91] In order to assess the educational inequalities faced by students based on their social origin; since each social class is characterised by a greater or lesser proximity to high culture valued by the school (see Chapter 2). In an article entitled "Les trois états du capital culturel,"[92] Pierre Bourdieu specifies that cultural capital can exist in three forms: the "embodied state" (p. 3), i.e. in the form of dispositions, knowledge and know-how that constitute a habitus (see Chapter 1); the "objectified state", in the form of cultural goods (pictures, books, dictionaries, instruments); and the "institutionalised state" in the form of educational qualifications.

- **Social Capital**
  Social capital is defined as "the aggregate of the actual or potential resources which are linked to the possession of a durable network of more or less institutionalised relationships of mutual acquaintance and recognition" ("Le capital social. Notes provisoires", 1980, p. 2)[93]. An agent's social capital is all the more significant when his network of relations is large and the people in his network are endowed with economic and cultural capital. Given that all the relations do not have the same value and certain relations prove to be more profitable than others, as a result, social capital has a multiplier effect when compared with other capitals: individuals obtain unequal returns on their economic or cultural capital depending on their greater or lesser capacity to mobilise their network and, by proxy, the capital of the members of the network.
- **Symbolic Capital**
  Symbolic capital deals with notions of prestige and social recognition. Pierre Bourdieu thus explains that "symbolic capital is nothing but economic capital or cultural capital that it is recognised and appreciated."[94] Having symbolic capital at one's disposal means having a certain influence over others who are prepared to offer respect.

The transmission and accumulation of capital, within a family or a social class, does not take place in the same way and depends on the type of capital that is taken into consideration:

- **Economic Capital**
  Being a material capital, the economic capital is transferred from one generation to the other simply through inheritance.
- **Cultural Capital**
  Cultural capital in the embodied state, in order to be

transmitted, involves a process of inculcation and assimilation that requires time. In the objectified state, cultural capital calls for the development of dispositions that help to appreciate the cultural goods that one possesses. Unlike economic capital, cultural capital disappears with its bearer. Nevertheless, the person who transmits it does not cease to possess it.

- **Social Capital**
  Social capital cannot be transmitted since it requires a continuous work of creation and maintenance in order to "produce and reproduce durable and useful networks, that help to procure material and symbolic benefits" ("Le capital social. Notes provisoires", 1980, p. 2). Thus social capital cannot be permanently attained and it requires, to remain effective, a periodic activation of one's contacts from the address book (like sending greetings cards at the beginning of the year).
- **Symbolic Capital**
  Symbolic capital is also subjected to accumulation strategies. Honour in pre-capitalist societies, or social prestige in contemporary societies are forms of symbolic capital that people seek to either preserve or increase. In *Le Sens pratique*,[95] Pierre Bourdieu cites the example of peasant families of Kabyle in the 1960s: "When a piece of land owned by a family since generations, falls into the hands of outsiders, repurchasing it becomes a matter of honour, comparable to revenge taken for an insult, and the price can become exorbitant." (p. 206) As a result, "protection of the 'symbolic' capital can [..] result in 'economically' disastrous behaviour" (p. 205).

Individuals and social classes are all equipped, to a greater or lesser degree, with each of these types of capital. Thus, there exists more than one form of inequality in society; as a matter of fact, there are as many types of inequalities as there are types of capital. The possession of different types of capital usually go in tandem with the emergence of overall inequalities.

- **Positions Within the Social Space**

Unlike Karl Marx, Pierre Bourdieu observes that the position of an individual in society is not solely determined by his position within the relations of production. The economic dimension is not the only criterion of positioning in the social space. Pierre Bourdieu also introduces "a break with the spontaneous representation of the social world that is summarised by the metaphor 'social ladder' "[96] and he substitutes it with the construction of a three-dimensional space. Like Max Weber, Bourdieu proposes a multidimensional concept of social space.

The position of an individual or of a class within the social space is defined by three elements that are defined in the order of their importance:

- **The Overall Capital Volume**

The overall capital volume refers to an individual's greater or lesser endowment of economic capital, cultural capital and social capital. People practising liberal professions who have higher incomes and higher educational qualifications and who entertain friends at home are thus positioned far away in the social space from industrial and agricultural workers with lower incomes, lacking educational qualifications and who entertain fewer guests.

- **The Capital Structure**

If the overall capital volume differentiates between the classes, it is the structure of the capital owned, or "structures of legacies" (*La Distinction*, p. 129), that subsequently distinguish between fractions of classes. The structure of the capital corresponds to the relative share of the economic capital on the one hand, and the cultural capital on the other, as these two types of capital are considered the main criteria of distinction in contemporary societies. Thus, in the social space, owners of commerce and industries, who own more economic capital than cultural capital, are placed opposite to professors, for whom the capital structure is the other way round. Professors relatively own more cultural capital and less economic capital compared to owners of commerce and industries. Pierre Bourdieu posits that economic capital is more indicative of a social class compared to cultural capital, since it is mainly concentrated in extremely closed environments that are less exposed to intergenerational mobility. The dominant class is thus divided, according to him, into a dominant fraction, characterised by a predominance of economic capital, and a dominated fraction, that is more endowed with cultural capital. Bourdieu explains that "given the fact that the volume of economic capital keeps increasing continuously while the volume of cultural capital decreases, as one moves from artists to owners of industries and commerce, it is observed that the dominant class develops in a *chiastic structure*" (*La Distinction*, p. 130). This chiastic structure, which states that the possession of economic capital is inversely proportional to the possession of cultural capital for the same overall volume of capital, is found at the level of the middle classes. In this case, the owners of mid-level industries and trade are positioned against school teachers. On the other hand, this structure does not exist within the popular classes who are first and foremost characterised by their low overall capital volume.

- **The Evolution of this Volume and This Structure Over Time**

  Pierre Bourdieu observes that time becomes the third structuring dimension of social space. The evolution of the volume and the structure of capital over time, depending on the ascending or descending social trajectory, contributes to the definition of the position of individuals and groups. The dominant fraction of the dominant class breaks down into two sub-groups: the traditional bourgeoisie, comprising owners of industries and trades, and the new bourgeoisie comprised by private sector executives. Their lifestyles differ based on the age or the duration of presence of the capital: while the new bourgeoisie denounces "the uptight severity of the old bourgeoisie who is straight-laced and preachy [..] the old bourgeoisie condemns the 'relaxed' lifestyle of the new bourgeoisie and insist on style and restraint when it comes to language and customs" (*La Distinction*, p. 358) (see Chapter 3). Likewise, due to their social trajectory, professors distinguish themselves from members of liberal professions, despite being endowed with the same level of cultural capital. Rising to the dominant class by the accumulation of educational capital, the professors are characterised by their ascetic aristocratism that leads them towards cultural practices that are "serious and even severe" (*La Distinction*, p. 325) such as reading, listening to classical music or visiting museums. Belonging to the bourgeois background, members of liberal professions exhibit luxurious tastes and collect the most expensive and most prestigious items ("going to concert halls, antique dealers and galleries, holidays in spa towns, possession of pianos"—*La Distinction*, p. 325).

Such a construction demonstrates a relational conception of social space: individuals and groups do not exist independently, their position is defined compared to the capital possessed by other individuals and groups. The notion of "space" is furthermore defined by Pierre Bourdieu as a "set of distinct and coexisting positions, external to each other, defined by each other, by their mutual exteriority and by relations of proximity, neighbourly relations or that of estrangement and also relations of position like above, below and between."[97]

Graphical Representation of Social Space

In order to give a synoptic view of the social space, Pierre Bourdieu conceives a schema of social positions and lifestyles space in "Anatomie du goût" (article co-authored with Monique de Saint-Martin[98]) and subsequently in *La Distinction*. Though the diagram does not aim to be "a crystal ball in which alchemists claimed to see at a glance everything happening in the world" (*La Distinction*, p. 139), this diagram aims to help understand the equivalence between spaces of social positions and lifestyle spaces (see Chapter 3). The following is a simplified version of the homology that was published in *Raisons pratiques. Sur la théorie de l'action:*[99]

The vertical axis in the diagram corresponds to the overall capital volume and the horizontal axis corresponds to the structure of this capital divided, according to a chiastic structure, between economic capital and cultural capital. The diagram thus summarises both the fundamental dimensions of the Bourdieusian social space. The social groups represented in bold type, are positioned according to the volume and the structure of their capital. The owners of trade and industries are placed on the north-east corner owing to the significance of their overall capital and the predominance of the economic capital within this capital. As for the working class, they are placed in the lower half of the schema due to the low volume of their total capital. The distance between the two groups on paper is representative of their social distance. The proximity between labourers and employees in the diagram demonstrates, on the contrary, a proximity between the structure and the volume of their capitals. The lifestyle space is then restored with the help of certain meaningful indicators (beverages, sports, musical instruments and board games). This space is added to the space defining

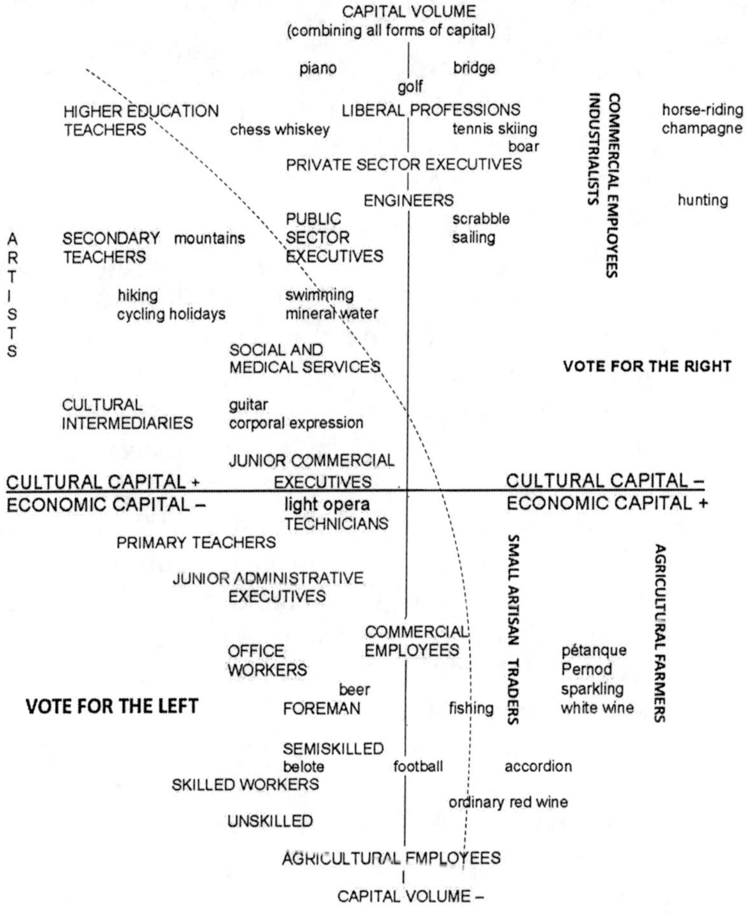

Social Positions and Lifestyles Space (*Raisons pratiques*, p. 21)

the positions in the schema in such a way that the proximities and distances between the social groups and practices become apparent. It is thus clear that the qualified working class play belote and football and the accordion more often than people practising liberal professions, i.e. the professionals. Since office clerical workers are closer to the labourers in the social space, they tend to share the same leisure activities. On the other hand, the professionals are more involved in activities such as bridge, golf or playing the piano. Finally, the crosscutting dotted lines indicate the line between the potential political orientation, either towards the right or the left.

This diagram emphasises the multidimensional and relational aspects of social space. Multidimensionality is represented by the two axes and the relational nature is established by the positioning of practices and groups in relation to each other. The proximities refer to the resemblances and the distances refer to disparities: "The spatial distances on paper are equivalent to social spaces" (*Raisons Pratiques*, p. 20).

Although the above schema does not correspond to a framework of factor analysis, its construction is partly a result of the study of results from multiple factor analyses by Pierre Bourdieu. Factor analysis is a statistical technique that helps to highlight the similarities and oppositions between the characteristics of the individuals studied. The factorial axes produced have to be analysed and interpreted in order to understand the meaning of these reconciliations and oppositions. The article "Anatomie du goût" (1976) constitutes the first application of the factor analysis method (or "geometric analysis of data") by Pierre Bourdieu and Monique de Saint-Martin. Pierre Bourdieu continues to use this method since it allows to establish a relational link to the social space.

Classification and Classification Struggles

Individuals who are closer to each other in the social space can be grouped together in the same social class. Each social class is characterised by a unique capital volume and structure. Social classes identified thus are not "real classes" but "classes on paper". In his article "Espace social et genèse des classes"[100] ('The Social Space and the Genesis of Groups'), Pierre Bourdieu is opposed to the Marxist theory, considered to be "realist", that tends to regard theoretical classes, i.e. classes conceived by the sociologist "on paper", as real classes which objectively exist and to which, groups of people get attached. That being said, Pierre Bourdieu also disagrees with the "nominalist" or "relativist" position that claims, on the contrary, that social classes have no substance in reality and are purely theoretical artefacts. In Bourdieu's opinion, social classes really exist from the moment they become subjects of political mobilisation, which basically creates a sense of belonging to the class: only a class that is "mobilised" can be considered to be a "real" class. Thereafter, Pierre Bourdieu's theory becomes discerning as it claims that "classes that can be segregated in the social space [...] do not exist as real groups even though they are likely to become practical groups, families (homogamy), clubs, associations and even labour or political 'movements'" (p. 4). A real class is more likely to emerge when it corresponds to a theoretical class, i.e. it brings together the agents who are objectively closer in the social space. In another text, "Espace social et espace symbolique" (*Raisons pratiques*, 1991) ('Social Space and Symbolic Space'), Pierre Bourdieu summarises his theory in the following manner: "What exists is a social space, a space of differences, classes exist within this space in a sort of virtual state, in the form of dotted lines, not as a given, but as *something that needs to be done.*" (p. 28)

Real classes, i.e. mobilised classes, are the result of classification struggles which explain the configuration of the social space. These political and symbolic struggles aim to establish a legitimate vision of the divisions in the social world. For Pierre Bourdieu, "the struggle over social classifications is a crucial dimension of the class struggle, and it is through this route that symbolic production intervenes in the political struggle. Classes exist twice over, once objectively, and a second time in the more or less explicit social representation that agents form of them, which is a stake in struggles."[101] In France, the socio-professional categories constructed by the INSEE (Institut national de la statistique et des études économiques) the National Institute of Statistics and Economic Studies, mould the perception of society: categories such as "executive", "labourer", "office clerk", etc. seem to be appropriate when it comes to classifying individuals according to their professional status and lifestyles. For Pierre Bourdieu, these socio-professional categories that officially control the legitimate vision of the social world, represent an act of symbolic representation by groups who are interested in imposing such a classification. It is because of their symbolic capital, acquired in the course of previous struggles, that these groups have an upper hand in class struggles. It is true that any perspective on divisions can only be imposed by agents who are best equipped in symbolic capital, i.e. the dominant classes.

By legitimising the social order which benefits them, the dominant classes exercise symbolic violence on the dominated classes (see Chapter 2). Once it is legitimised, domination actually appears to be "natural" not only to the dominating classes but also to the dominated, who are unaware of the mechanisms of imposition of this arbitrary. For instance, the socio-professional categories are accepted by everyone in France. The invisible nature of domination depends on the production of non-explicit beliefs that form the *doxa*, that is, a common opinion that is shared and not questioned. This *doxa* prevents the realisation of domination. Pierre Bourdieu explains that: "The legitimisation of the social world is not, as some believe, the product of a deliberate and purposive action of propaganda or symbolic imposition; it results rather, from the fact that agents apply to the objective structures of the social world structures of perception and appreciation which are issued out of these very structures which tend to picture the world as evident."[102] Consequently, following the principle of *amor fati* (see Chapter 2), the dominated classes adhere to their own domination and tend to adapt their subjective expectations to the objective probabilities of their social success, by convincing themselves that certain positions are not made for them. The legitimised social order is maintained by the strength of symbolic violence: that is social reproduction (see Chapter 2).

In certain instances, there may nevertheless exist a gap between the proposed objective chances and the realistic aspirations founded on a previous state of objective chances. This is the case when an individual or a group has experienced an interrupted trajectory, that is, a decline in relation to the potential objective trajectory that the earlier state had expected. In this case, individuals and families seek to fight against classification. To this end, they depend on the ability to convert their capitals and to implement regeneration strategies: "The *conversion* of capital, owned in one particular form into another more accessible, more profitable, more legitimate form, in a given state of the system of instruments of reproduction, tends to induce a transformation in the structure of assets." (*La Distinction*, p. 145) The goal is to protect the overall volume of capital. Pierre Bourdieu cites the example of the "members of the new petty-bourgeoisie originally from the upper classes who (most often), due to the lack of academic capital are forced to undergo a professional conversion and they choose new professions, such as that of a cultural intermediary or craftsperson." (*La Distinction*, p. 416): their family-owned cultural capital is not converted into academic capital, nevertheless, their engagement in semi-bourgeois positions saves them from a drop in status. However, since all the classes struggle to achieve a better social position, the hierarchy between the classes is not disturbed. People simply experience a shift upwards, from their individual positions, in the course of time, which does not affect the structure of the hierarchy. Considering the social space relationally thus moderates the impact of social change.

1.2 The Function of the Concept of Capital
(François de Singly, 1987)

Pierre Bourdieu's works on the concept of "capital" led to other researches, where sociologists subsequently used the concept of "capital" to analyse the resources available to individuals and study the strategies aimed at increasing them. In *Fortune et infortune de la femme mariée. Sociologie de la vie conjugale*[103] ('A Married Woman's Fortune and Misfortune'), a book that stems from a doctoral thesis defended in 1984 under the supervision of Alain Girard, François de Singly questions the manner in which conjugal life alters the way a woman manages her cultural, economic and social capital. He revisits the economic concept of "capital" in order to assess a subject that is inherently foreign to any branch of economics: marriage. Trained in the Bourdieusian school of thought, François de Singly is currently professor in the Université de Paris Descartes and director of CERLIS (Centre de recherche sur les liens sociaux) Research Centre for Social Links, where he conducts research on family and education.

Capital and the Marriage Market

In *Fortune et infortune de la femme mariée* (1987), François de Singly proposes "a fiction on conjugal life" (p. 7) which strays from the subject of love, to focus on costs and returns associated with marriage, for a man as well as for a woman. Francois de Singly uses a vocabulary related to economics, evoking concepts such as cost, returns as well as concepts of market, of capital, etc., to analyse the sacred subject of marriage, that one usually refuses to assess in economic terms. He justifies his method of analysis in the following manner: "In order to obtain a different vision of conjugal life, I adjust my sociological lenses in such a way that the love that unites the spouses remains in a state of flux. On the other hand, this exclusion helps to perceive a dimension that is most often concealed: the social interests which are at stake in contemporary families" (p. 8). By deliberately resorting to oversimplification, he considers that the social value of an individual can be measured by taking into account his overall capital. In order to yield a profit, the entirety of his capital should be placed either in the job market or in the marriage market.

The author highlights a set of statistical results based on the secondary analysis of surveys conducted by the INSEE. He showed, in particular, that many marriages do not observe homogamy, that is, union between individuals of similar social origins. In fact, the choice of a spouse reveals that there exists an affinity between the volumes of capital of the man and the woman but these capitals are not similar in nature. Thus, most often the man offers his economic capital in exchange for the aesthetic or social capital of the woman. As a result, the marital union expands the capital volume of each individual. However, the return on educational capital (called "educational dowry") for the man and the woman varies, as they are reversed after marriage, compared to unmarried individuals. Married men get a better return on their qualification compared to unmarried men, while married women obtain a poor output on their qualification compared to unmarried women. The unequal distribution of domestic chores post marriage and the birth of children might explain this result. François de Singly concludes that "marriage is a bad deal for women in terms of their professional life" (p. 76).

Unmarried women, who do not have to worry about the domestic needs of a husband, often have prestigious professions when compared to married women. Conversely, unmarried men, most often, have agricultural jobs or lower positions in the organisational hierarchy, compared to married men. This creates an imbalance of capitals in the matrimonial market: unmarried women have more economic and educational capital at their disposal than unmarried men, which reduces the probability of their union. Based on their educational capital, men and women are therefore unequal when it comes to conjugal life and its impact.

Economic Concepts to Explain a Sociological Reality

The systematic use of a vocabulary related to economics by François de Singly as well as his strategic reading of statistics have been criticised;[104] just as Pierre Bourdieu was reproached for his use of economic analogies. Terms such as capital, interest, inflation, etc., actually suggest that he offers an "economic" view of the social world. Pierre Bourdieu himself is not only critical of the philosophy behind the field of economics but also of sociologists who use it as the foundation of their theory, like the American economist Gary Becker who states that all action is the fruit of an economic calculation. In fact, the use of terms related to economics allows Pierre Bourdieu to highlight features that are common to different social universes: the notion of capital can, for example, be transposed to economic, cultural, political universes. The sociologist thus seeks to objectify the social world and specifically the universes that resist this objectification, such as the literary world. The introduction of the concept of "field" also allows him to propose the same explanatory system for different domains of social life.

2. THE THEORY OF FIELDS

According to Pierre Bourdieu, the social space is made up of a plurality of social spaces such as the artistic field, the economic field, the journalistic field, the political field, the religious field, the educational field or even the field of sports. The theory of fields conceived by Pierre Bourdieu is meant to identify similarities in the structure and functioning of different domains of social life.

2.1 Field and Position within the Field

The concept of "field", employed to describe the social world, first emerges in the world of Pierre Bourdieu in 1966 ("Champ intellectuel et projet créateur"[105]). Pierre Bourdieu defines fields as spheres of the social world which have become independent, thanks to the process of progressive differentiation of the social world owing to the increase in the division of labour. The autonomy of the social field is achieved once the central stake of each field is clearly defined. For instance, the central stake of the political field is power. That of the field of economics is wealth, and of the artistic field is recognition. Individuals who want to partake in a field, act according to the stakes involved in that field. Thus in the field of literature, the specific form of capital is established by peer recognition which is materialised for example, in the form of literary prizes. The possession of this particular capital determines one's position within the field. Just like the social space, a field can be described as a space comprising positions and relations between the positions of the different participants. The history of struggles involving the acquisition or the preservation of specific capital materialises within the field in the form of regulations or institutions (for example, titles of nobility, deeds of property or educational qualifications) that enable the field to perpetuate.

The Game Metaphor

Pierre Bourdieu uses the game metaphor in order to describe the functioning of fields: each field has its own playing rules which constitute its orthodoxy. The playing rules of a particular field define the legitimate mechanisms of acquisition and preservation of the capital that are specific to that field. These mechanisms, for example, comprise rules for recruitment which determine the conditions that allow an individual to enter the field (like defending a thesis to enter into the academic field) or rituals of recognition that elevate his position within the field (like receiving a literary prize for a writer).

The analogy between the field and the game is explored even further. According to Pierre Bourdieu, what helps to sustain a field is "the collective adhesion to the game which constitutes both the cause and effect of the existence of the game."[106] For the game to exist, it is important for the players to believe in it, to believe in the value of the stakes and in the advantage of playing for that stake. Pierre Bourdieu calls *illusio* the phenomenon of "being caught up and by the game, of believing that the game is worthwhile, or, simply put, that it is worth playing") (*Raisons pratiques*, 1994, p. 151). The Latia term *illusio* comes from *ludus*, which means "game". This word lays emphasis on the illusion or the apparent absurdity experienced by those who remain outside the game and the interest generated by the game. In *Raisons Pratiques* (1994), Pierre Bourdieu cites the example of a sculpture, in the Auch Cathedral, which represents two monks struggling over the prior's staff. For someone outside the religious field, this staff has no value and the struggle may seem ludicrous and baseless. However, the monks who are a part of the religious field can see its importance. Even in a field such as the religious universe that preaches disinterest, its participants can identify an interest in struggling over certain possessions.

The internalisation of the *illusio,* particular to a given field, can be done by acquiring a habitus that is aligned with the field. In fact, the "magical relationship with a game [..] is the product of an ontological complicity between mental and objective structures of the social space" (*Raisons Pratiques,* p. 151). Habitus helps to internalise the knowledge and recognition of the stakes and the laws of the field. In the educational field for example, students who succeed are those who, within their families, were the best prepared to meet the expectations of the school. They acquired, without knowing it, an educational habitus that predisposes them to spontaneously feel at ease in school and to know what they need to do to succeed. In other words, they instantly know how to "play" in this field.

Habitus thus enables practices to adjust themselves spontaneously according to the requirements of the field, without making its agents consciously calculate its interest. It is in this way that the (objective) success of certain individuals in a field can be accounted for without first considering it as the result of a conscious (subjective) quest for profit. Pierre Bourdieu thus writes: "Habitus [..] is a generator of strategies that can be objectively compatible with the objective interests of their creators even though they were not conceived for this purpose" (*Questions de sociologie,* pp. 119-120).

Field of Forces, Field of Struggles

If each field has its specific features (its stakes, its particular type of capital, its rules) that make it irreducible to other fields, there also exists general laws that apply to all the fields. Pierre Bourdieu warns against "the mistake of inventing as many explanatory systems as there are fields instead of seeing each of them as a transformed form of all the others; or worse, the error of setting up a particular combination of factors active in a particular field of practices as a universal explanatory principle" (*La Distinction*, p. 127). It is, on the contrary, necessary to look for what the different fields have in common. According to the author, these are the relationships that are established between positions inside a field. These relationships can bc explored in two ways. From a static perspective, a field is a force field. At a given time, a field is characterised by an unequal distribution of resources which determines the different positions. Broadly speaking, in every field, there are individuals rich in a specific capital who become the dominants, and there are the less well endowed who are dominated. According to Pierre Bourdieu, "those who dominate the field have the means to make it function to their advantage; but they have to reckon with the resistance of the dominated agents" ("Le capital social. Notes provisoires", 1980). Unequal endowment creates a power relationship between the dominant and the dominated agents. Subsequently, the positions of the agents acquire meaning only in relation to each other: they only exist relationally. Each position is defined by the quantity of specific capital accumulated by the agent during the course of previous struggles. Thus from a dynamic perspective, the field becomes a field of struggles. The agents confront each other in this field (with resources that depend on their position within the force field) with a view to preserve or transform the initial relation of force and therefore the structure of the field. The existence of social struggles within each specialised field does not permit, like the Marxist theory, the discourse on a unique and central conflict that structures the whole society.

Strategies of Struggle

Confrontations within fields manifest themselves through stances that agents take around the stakes involved in a field, for instance, the right or the left political stance of agents in the political field. These stances adopted by agents in the struggle depend on the position of the agents in the field and their trajectory. In fact, it is in part the position which determines the stance. The position within the field instantly defines the "point of view" of the agents. It is from this point of view that representations of struggles and their respective stakes are forged. Habitus, which is at the origin of a homology between objective and mental structures, explains this convergence between a position and a stance. The trajectory (ascending or descending) of individuals is another element that structures their dispositions and representations, and consequently, their stances. These stances can be interpreted as the result of strategies (not necessarily conscious) designed to preserve or improve the agent's position. Pierre Bourdieu assumes that agents' actions are always directed towards the preservation or the elevation of their position in the social space.

Pierre Bourdieu defines two major types of strategies: conservation strategies and subversion strategies. The first type, also called reproduction or succession strategies, are strategies employed by individuals who monopolise a specific capital of the field and seek to preserve or improve their position by perpetuating the game which turns in their favour. These are the defenders of orthodoxy, of the game just as it is. Their dominant position allows them to establish the game rules that are most favourable to their interests. At the other end, the upholders of subversion strategies are individuals who are less endowed with a specific capital. These are often new entrants who come across as "aspirants". They are considered to be heretics since they challenge the legitimacy of the hierarchy of positions inside the field by trying to change the rules of the game or the very nature of the stakes of the field, in order to re-evaluate their capital, and in the process, improve their position. The agents who are excluded or those who are poorly positioned in the field can try, for instance, to expand the institutional or symbolic boundaries of the field in order to participate in the field or reassert the value of their position.

In "Le couturier et sa griffe: contribution à une théorie de la magie"[107] ('The Fashion Designer and His Signature: Contribution to a Theory of Magic'), Pierre Bourdieu and Yvette Delsaut describe the strategies of conservation and subversion that were at work in the field of haute couture at the turn of the twentieth century. In order to obtain "the monopoly of specific legitimacy [in the field of fashion], that is, [..] the exclusive power to constitute and impose the legitimate symbols of distinction in regard to clothing" (p. 15), young designers confronted established designers. To "create fashion", the new entrants in the field question the existing aesthetic norms and conventions. They try to make them appear outdated by introducing for instance, colour combinations and original materials. By doing so, they tend to not only "put out of fashion the fashion of the year before" but also "strip [those who created the fashion of the year before] of their authority over fashion" (p. 15). In response, the heirs of large fashion houses adopt strategies to preserve their capital especially by trying to convert their symbolic capital into economic capital. The stances, aesthetic as well as commercial strategies, adopted within the field of fashion, thus depend on the position inside the structure of distribution of the specific capital.

Limitations of the Struggle

Although every individual involved in a field struggles to either preserve or improve his position, this struggle is nevertheless defined by an interest which is common to everyone. It is a question of the very existence of the field. In fact, "among people who occupy opposing positions in a field and who seem radically opposed in everything, there is a hidden and tacit accord about the fact that it is worth the effort to struggle for the things that are in play in the field" (*Raisons Pratiques*, p. 152). The struggle assumes, just as Simmel[108] demonstrates, a minimal accord, among the participants, about what merits to be the object of the struggle. This accord (which comes under the *doxa*) remains implicit, but it is the condition that permits entry into the game. Consequently, the strategies of subversion are always limited. According to Pierre Bourdieu, they cannot lead to "*partial revolutions* [who] do not call into question the very foundations of the game, its fundamental axioms, the bedrock of ultimate beliefs on which the whole game is based" (*Questions de sociologie*, p. 116).

Although incapable of questioning the foundations of the game, an opposition is a necessity for the existence of the field, since the defenders of orthodoxy need the existence of a heresy in order to reaffirm the *doxa*. As a result, behind their antagonism there is an underlying "objective complicity" that links all the individuals.

Structural Homology Between Fields

The structural homology between the fields, i.e. their structural similarity, is consubstantial with the definition of the field which states that it is a space determined by the relative positions between the people, who are more or less endowed with a specific capital. There is, in particular, a homology between the field of production in a domain (for instance the social space of designers of haute couture) and the field of reception in the same domain (that of the clients of haute-couture). In the case of fashion, Pierre Bourdieu and Yvette Delsaut (1975) show that the logic of internal struggles in the field of production (the opposition between established designers and new designers) correspond to the logic of internal struggles in the field of the clients (opposition between the dominant fractions and the dominated fractions of the dominant classes). In the 1960s, while the dominated fractions opted for products of new upcoming designers (Courrèges), the dominant fractions moved towards the older fashion houses (Dior). The similarity of their position within the respective fields ensures that manufacturers and consumers are "structurally attuned [...] in their vision of the social world, their tastes and their entire habitus" (*La Distinction,* p. 267). This is "the logic of homologies, and not cynical calculation, which causes works to be adjusted to the expectations of their audience" (*La Distinction,* p. 266).

The structural homology between the field of manufacturers and consumers explains the success of ready to wear garments at the turn of the twentieth century: this "revolution" in the field of fashion, the product of innovative technics and a stylistic reorientation, was extremely successful, since it met the expectations of the women of the new bourgeoisie who were in search for practical and refined clothing for work.

Static Field and Field of Power: Meta-Fields

In the bourdieusian theory, the static field occupies a special position compared to the other fields. The specific capital of the state, which is a symbolic capital, is defined as a "meta-capital" since it is formed by the concentration of different types of capital (military capital, economic capital, cultural capital...). It is this concentration of capital that gives the state authority over the other fields. While Max Weber spoke about the state's monopoly on "legitimate physical violence", Pierre Bourdieu opines that the state holds the monopoly of "legitimate symbolic violence". In his opinion, the state possesses the "legal power of nomination, that is, the power to officially impose a legitimate vision of the social world" ("Espace social et genèse des classes", 1984). This enables the state to impose its principles of (di-)vision of the social world through institutions charged with legitimising (expert assessment), inculcating (school) and enforcing (justice) them. Within this framework, politics is viewed as the struggle to impose a legitimate vision of the social world. The outcome of the struggles that take place within the political field are legitimised by the state. In addition to this cognitive action, the state can, thanks to the material and symbolic resources that it accumulates, regulate the functioning of different fields through financial interventions (for example, through public aid for investment in the economic field) or legal interventions (delineation of laws) which help to define the power relations between capital owners. The state is thus a meta-field, not only because it absorbs the different fields (and each field becomes the state's domain of specialisation: education, culture, economics) but also because it integrates itself into the fields when defining the rules and mechanisms of allocation of resources for the fields.

Although linked to the field of the state, the field of power enjoys a certain degree of autonomy. Pierre Bourdieu defines the field of power as "the space defining the power relations between agents or between institutions with common interest in acquiring the capital necessary to occupy dominant positions in different fields (especially economic or cultural)."[109] The field of power is thus a field of a struggle between the dominant groups of different fields "for the imposition of the *dominant principle of domination* [...] [which] is also a struggle over the *legitimate principle of legitimation* and, inseparably, the legitimate mode of reproduction of the foundations of domination."[110] The field of power thus emerges as the field of all fields, at the source of the hierarchy between the different fields. The dominant agents of each field have, besides the strategies of reproduction, "symbolic strategies that aim to legitimise the social foundation of their domination" (p. 377) by ensuring that the superiority of their specific capital, that establishes their power, is acknowledged. The objective hierarchy of the different forms of capital, especially economic and cultural, determines the distribution of different fields within the field of power. In *La Noblesse d'État* (1989) where he studies the structure of the field of power, Pierre Bourdieu highlights the following hierarchy: at the summit of the field of power, lies the economic field, followed by the administrative and the academic fields and finally the artistic field. The struggle within the field of power also includes the struggle of power over the state, but it is not limited to it: the domination of the dominant agents of other fields by the dominant agents of the economic field, does not necessarily involve the state.

2.2 The Use of the Concept of Field: Example of the Literary Field (Pierre Bourdieu, 1992; Christophe Charle, 1977)

Various fields have been studied in the works of Pierre Bourdieu: the literary field (*Les Règles de l'art*, 1992), the economic field through the market of single-family detached homes (*Les Structures sociales de l'économie*, 2000)[111], the field of haute-couture ("Le couturier et sa griffe", 1975), the religious field ("Genèse et structure du champ religieux," 1971[112]), the field of the employers ("Le patronat", 1978[113]), the field of the grandes écoles or elite higher education institutes and the field of power (*La Noblesse d'État*, 1989). In all the cases, Pierre Bourdieu observes that in order to study a field, it is necessary to trace the genesis of the field (the method of genetic structuralism, see Chapter 1). It is a question of observing how a domain of the social world gradually separates itself from the other domains and becomes independent.

The Literary Field Studied by Pierre Bourdieu

In *Les Règles de l'art. Genèse et structure du champ littéraire* (1992), Pierre Bourdieu studies the constitution of the literary field at the end of the nineteenth century, its relations with the other fields, the birth of its unique stakes and the simultaneous creation of its agents' dispositions. The autonomy of a field is defined by the ability of the field to establish its own quality assessment criterion, without referring to an exogenous criterion. The autonomy of the literary field at the end of the nineteenth century consisted of replacing the ethical, political and most importantly, the commercial criteria that were in force till then and were used to assess the quality of literary works, with a criterion of an aesthetic nature defined by the judgement of literary peers. This gave rise to an actual "symbolic revolution" since the literary world reversed the order of the values that prevailed in the economic field. Economic success, was no longer a measure of value, instead, it would be seen as a negative indicator of literary quality: the genuine artist would henceforth have a selfless striving for art and would only make art "for art's sake". The study of the construction of fields traces the struggle which led to the implementation of the endogenous criterion for the assessment of quality.

The struggle for the "imposition of the legitimate definition of a writer" (p. 311) saw the emergence of two opposite poles within the literary field. The first is the commercial large-scale production pole, the makers of popular entertainment, catering to the general public. This pole views literature as a business like any other, where writers aspire to achieve instant commercial success (by producing *bestsellers,* for instance). The key to success for authors is thus exogenous as it involves the economic criterion. The second pole is that of pure art, involving small-scale or restricted production and corresponding to the avant-garde current. Artistic works are regarded for their aesthetic value by the artistic world itself. The artists, who do not receive instant recognition, aspire to achieve posterity, through their works which would go on to become "classics". In this case, the legitimate principle of hierarchisation of works comes from within the field: the commercial aspect is denied and rejected, selflessness is established as a value system with the ambition to achieve autonomy in relation to other fields of the social world. These two fields—pure and commercial—bring together authors, who have nothing in common (in terms of literary production, readership, social circles), except the struggle for the definition of the boundaries of the field.

Literary Field and Field of Power (Christophe Charle, 1977)

Christophe Charle is a historian. Director of the Institut d'Histoire Moderne et Contemporaine and professor at the University of Paris I—Panthéon-Sorbonne, the works of this former member of the CSE (Centre de sociologie européenne) is greatly inspired by the Bourdieusian theory.

In "Champ littéraire et champ du pouvoir. Les écrivains et l'Affaire Dreyfus,"[114] he shows that the use of the concept of field helps to assess the political stances taken by the French writers during the Dreyfus affair. This socio-historical approach is relatively new since it overlooks the descriptions that revolve around the personalities of the protagonists, the symbolic aspect of the events and the emotions that were aroused.

The positions taken by the writers, for or against the re-hearing of the Alfred Dreyfus trial (a captain in the French army of Jewish descent, wrongly convicted for divulging military secrets to the Germans in 1895) cannot be reduced to their political opinions or their social properties. Individuals have to be placed within the literary field and their relations with the political field have to be simultaneously studied in order to understand what led the writers to take a stand on the issue and force the political figures to reorganise themselves based on the divisions they had created.

Christophe Charle distinguished three poles within the literary field at the end of the nineteenth century. The position occupied by each of the three poles and the relations they maintained with the political field are conditions that explain the stances taken by the members. The dominant pole is that of literature with institutional recognition (like the position of writers who belong to the Académie française). In the literary field, this pole aims to maintain the established order with the intention of preserving its position. In order to do so, it supports "legitimate" literature as it is confronted by challenges from new schools, such as naturalism or avant-garde poetry. This conservative position is transferred to the political field: the academic pole of literature is largely anti-dreyfusard since it stands against the re-hearing of the trial which exonerated Alfred Dreyfus and thereby threatened the established order and the authority of the army.

At the other end, i.e. the dominated pole of literature, comprising mainly of the poetic avant-garde (that has its own unique criteria of evaluating literary quality), was behind the initiative for the proposal to reopen the case: Bernard Lazare, a journalist who was responsible for publicising the case, was head of a symbolist review. Christophe Charle highlights the homology between the dominated condition of the poetic avant-garde in the literary field and the dominant nature of dreyfusism, at the time of its emergence, in the political field. He observes that it is the same refusal to compromise with public taste in the literary field and with justice in the political field, in the name of autonomy of the individual, that mobilised the members of this fraction of the literary field. The problem lies in the fact that these individuals, due to their dominated position in the field, are too marginal to have any political weight. They have to therefore depend on the third fraction of the field, the intermediate pole, to voice their views.

The intermediate pole of the literary field is that of the popular novel and boulevard theatre that cater to the general public. This pole was initially the most divided and the least involved in the Dreyfus affair. Due to the support offered by the state to bourgeois theatre its playwrights stayed away from political discourse except when they were motived by personal gain. However, only such writers, owing to their position in the field, "are capable of playing the dual role of defending an ideology and liaising with the political field" (p. 252). This is the reason why the rallying cry of support extended to Dreyfus by Émile Zola, who belonged to this pole (while also occupying a dominant position that was rejected by the other dominant agents, because of his popular success), is important. His popular appeal and his proximity to the political circles (since he was a writer and journalist) allowed him to start the debate outside the literary field. With the publication of his article "J'accuse...!", everyone took positions around the question: "by launching the debate outside the limited scope of the parliamentary precinct and pointless traditional disputes and by introducing a rift in values that are ideological and literary to begin with (Truth, Justice), Zola compelled the entire literary field to be concerned" (p. 253). He led the rally to defend Alfred Dreyfus and all those whose socio-cultural backgrounds predisposed them to feel dominated. Alfred Dreyfus' conviction was eventually called into question and the captain was finally exonerated and reinstated.

Thus Christophe Charle concludes that there is a homology between positions in the literary field and stances taken in the political field. Using the Bourdieusian concept, he highlights how changes in power relations within the literary field have implications on the formulation of stakes in the political field.

2.3 From the Economic Field to the Economy of Symbolic Goods

The Social Construction of the Economic Field

The economic field was thoroughly examined by Pierre Bourdieu, especially in his later writings. The accusations of "economism" due to the use of economic analogies (see part 1 of this chapter), compels him to clarify his link with the economic discipline. Staying true to his epistemological position articulated in *Le Métier de sociologue*[115] (see Chapter 1), Pierre Bourdieu believes that the work of the sociologist is to denaturalise "all that the economic discipline presents as a given,"[116] that is, the economic institutions (especially the market) but also economic dispositions (such as the calculating rationality). This constructivist approach is presently a preferred approach in the field of economic sociology which constitutes a dynamic branch of sociology, and owes to Pierre Bourdieu for being one of its initiators. His book published in the year 2000, *Les Structures sociales de l'économie*, is an emblematic case study of such an approach. In this book, Bourdieu highlights all the social processes necessary for the establishment of the single-family detached houses market. This market is "the product of a *dual social construction*, to which the state makes an important contribution" (p. 30): construction of the demand (coming from the consumers), on the one hand, and construction of the supply (suggested by the builders), on the other hand. The construction of the demand reflects the shaping of individual preferences, especially in terms of property and rentals. The allocation of government aid to construction and housing, through different laws and regulations, contributes to the increased demand of single-family detached houses. The construction of the offer also relies on the state's policy which, by granting specific funds to the builders of single-family detached houses, redefines the position of each of these builders inside the market which is conceived as a field. Pierre Bourdieu finally emphasises the need to recreate the genesis of the economic field: by tracing the history of processes such as differentiation and autonomisation, which enables the field to construct its own specific stakes and laws, the sociologist calls into question the validity of the hypothesis which states that the economic field would be a universe, that is, in essence, separate from other areas of life. By doing so, he challenges the epistemological process specific to economics.

In an article entitled "La fabrique de l'habitus économique"[117] ("Making the Economic Habitus"), Pierre Bourdieu further explains that the economic arrangements that are made for the agents (based on a rationale that relies on calculation and maximisation) are not natural but cultural, and thus are not universally valid. Based on his field study conducted in the 1960s in colonised Kabyle (in Algeria), he writes: "The discordance between economic arrangements made in a pre-capitalist economy and the economic cosmos imported and imposed, sometimes in the most brutal manner, through colonisation, forced to see that access to the most elementary economic behaviours (salaried job, savings, credit, population planning, etc.) is not self-evident and the so-called "rational" economic agent is the product of unique historical conditions." (p. 79) Speaking of the "economic habitus", is to emphasise the historicity of these arrangements that constitute the *homo œconomicus* valued by economists. By studying the transformation of the economic practices in Kabyle in the 1960s, Pierre Bourdieu brings to light the emergence of a "system of beliefs" in the Algerian rural society. The study of the genesis of the economic habits led him to consider that economics can be analysed as a "system of beliefs".

Economic Reasoning, Symbolic Reasoning

Questioning the universality of economic rationality allows Pierre Bourdieu to highlight other approaches of action adopted by individuals, within the economic field itself. He intends to "wrest from economism (Marxist or neomarginalist) pre-capitalist economies and entire sectors of so-called capitalist economies which do not function according to the law of interest seen as the search for the maximisation of (monetary) profit." (*Raisons Pratiques*, p. 176). In order to do so, he focuses specially on certain spheres of social life, which despite being sites of exchange associated with value-creation, reject the principles of economics. Pierre Bourdieu especially studies the artistic universe, the domestic economy, the religious sphere and the bureaucracy. In these spaces, the validation of the symbolic ("prestige", "authority") go hand in hand with the "denial of economics". In the artistic field, for example, instant success, which corresponds to the great sale of artistic works and rapid monetary gains by artists, is considered as a negative indicator of the artistic value of the creator. A person is all the more valued and recognised when he seems to be disinterested in economic gains; economic altruism being a necessary condition for the accumulation of symbolic capital. This accumulated symbolic capital can eventually be transformed into economic capital. Such is the case of the accursed artists whose works, in the long term, gained substantial economic profits. Thus ironically, individuals have a great deal to "gain from their disinterestedness". According to Pierre Bourdieu, this disinterest is neither a pure rejection of interest (because ultimately, there is a symbolic profit earned from being disinterested), nor is it a concealment of interest (since individuals sincerely adhere to this logic). This disposition is the result of the functioning of the field itself: "For the alchemy to function, as in the exchange of gifts, it has to be sustained by the entire social structure, therefore by the mental structures and disposition produced by that social structure; there must be a market for like symbolic actions, there must be rewards, symbolic profits, often convertible into material profit, people must be able to have an interest in disinterestedness" (p. 186). Economic interest must be continuously euphemised ("the taboo on explicitation"). This is achieved, in particular by constructing a discourse that hides the "economic truth" behind every action. Thus, in the religious world, priests do not talk of a "salaried work" but about "sacred service", they do not use the word "customers" but talk of the "faithful". This discourse should not be understood as an ideology that is meant to conceal hypocritical practices: it forms an integral part of the very functioning of the economy of symbolic goods. As a result, it must be taken seriously as such by economic sociologists.

Pierre Bourdieu's interest in the economy of symbolic goods offers a fresh perspective on the question of the production of value. He especially highlights the originality of the mechanisms of production of symbolic value. This value is not, in fact, inherent in the goods or the result of pure market mechanisms: it is produced by the "institutions of consecration", such as art dealers, editors or critics in the artistic field. The latter act as "symbolic banker[s]"[118] who transfer their own legitimacy to a work of art in order to sanction it. Hence, a book edited in a prestigious publishing house benefits from the symbolic capital that the publisher has in the literary world. Similarly, a fabricator, once established, legitimises in return all his new productions, simply by signing them: "The signature [...], without changing the material of the product, transforms it into a luxury product, altering at once, its economic and symbolic value" ("Le couturier et sa griffe", p. 21). This "*symbolic transubstantiation* process, irreducible to a material transformation" (p. 21) has been interpreted by Pierre Bourdieu, in the last analysis, as a magical phenomenon arising from the functioning of the field itself: "The almost magical potency of the signature is nothing other than the power, bestowed on certain individuals, to mobilise the symbolic energy produced by the functioning of the entire field, that is, the faith in the game and the stakes produced by the game itself" ("La production de la croyance", p. 9). Pierre Bourdieu's interest in the economy of symbolic goods thus opens new avenues of the sociological analysis of economic activities.

NOTES

91. Bourdieu, P. et Passeron, J.-C., *La Reproduction. Éléments pour une théorie du système d'en- seignement* (1970), Paris, Minuit.

92. "Les trois états du capital culturel", *Actes de la Recherche en Sciences Sociales* (1979), Vol. 30, pp. 3-6.
93. "Le capital social. Notes provisoires", *Actes de la Recherche en Sciences Sociales* (1980), Vol. 31, pp. 2-3.
94. *Choses dites* (1987), Paris, Minuit, p. 160.
95. *Le Sens pratique* (1980), Paris, Minuit.
96. *La Distinction. Critique sociale du jugement* (1979), Paris, Minuit, p. 137.
97. "Espace social et espace symbolique", in *Raisons pratiques. Sur la théorie de l'action* (1994), Paris, Seuil, pp. 13-29, citation p. 20.
98. Bourdieu, P. et Saint-Martin (de), M., "Anatomie du goût", *Actes de la Recherche en Sciences Sociales* (1976), Vol. 2, pp. 2-81.
99. *Raisons pratiques. Sur la théorie de l'action* (1994), Paris, Seuil.
100. "Espace social et genèse des classes", *Actes de la Recherche en Sciences Sociales* (1984), Vol. 52, pp. 3-14.
101. *Questions de sociologie* (1984), Paris, Minuit, p. 62.
102. "Espace social et pouvoir symbolique", in *Choses dites* (1987), Paris, Minuit, pp. 147-166, citation pp. 160-161.
103. Singly (de), F., *Fortune et infortune de la femme mariée. Sociologie de la vie conjugale* (1987), Paris, Presses Universitaires de France.
104. Héran, F., "Compte-rendu de : de Singly François. 1987. Fortune et infortune de la femme mariée, PUF", *Revue française de sociologie* (1987), Vol. 28, No. 4.
105. "Champ intellectuel et projet créateur", *Les Temps modernes* (1966), No. 246, pp. 865-906.
106. *Les Règles de l'art. Genèse et structure du champ littéraire* (1992), Paris, Seuil, p. 279.
107. Bourdieu, P., Delsaut, Y., "Le couturier et sa griffe : contribution à une théorie de la magie", *Actes de la Recherche en Sciences Sociales* (1975), Vol. 1, pp. 7-36.
108. Simmel, G., *Le Conflit* (1995, [1908]), Paris, Circé.
109. "Le champ littéraire", *Actes de la Recherche en Sciences Sociales* (1991), Vol. 89, pp. 3-46.
110. *La Noblesse d'État. Grandes écoles et esprit de corps* (1989), Paris, Minuit, p. 376.
111. *Les Structures sociales de l'économie* (2000), Paris, Seuil.
112. "Genèse et structure du champ religieux", *Revue française de sociologie* (1971), Vol. 12, pp. 295-334.

113. "Le patronat", *Actes de la Recherche en Sciences Sociales* (1978), Vol. 20, pp. 3-82.
114. Charle, C., "Champ littéraire et champ du pouvoir. Les écrivains et l'Affaire Dreyfus", *Annales* (1977), Vol. 32, No. 2, pp. 240-264.
115. Bourdieu, P., Chamboredon, J.-C. et Passeron, J.-C., *Le Métier de sociologue : préalables épistémologiques* (1968), Paris, Mouton.
116. *Les Structures sociales de l'économie* (2000), Paris, Seuil, p. 16.
117. "La fabrique de l'habitus économique", *Actes de la Recherche en Sciences Sociales* (2003), No. 150, pp. 79-90.
118. "La production de la croyance. Contribution à une économie des biens symboliques", *Actes de la Recherche en Sciences Sociales* (1977), Vol. 13, No. 1, pp. 3-43, citation p. 6.

Conclusion

Pierre Bourdieu developed the general theory of the social world which renewed the ways of thinking and practising sociology. Certain domains, such as the sociology of education and cultural sociology, have been profoundly transformed by the Bourdieusian framework of thought. Pierre Bourdieu's theory is based on an epistemological reflection that highlights the need, for sociologists, to adopt a reflective process when it comes to the methods they used. His theory is also based on key concepts—notably the theory of habitus and the theory of fields—conceived to surpass classical oppositions between objectivism and subjectivism or between macro sociology and micro sociology. These concepts are specifically identified today as Bourdieusian. Both the theory of social reproduction and the general economy of practice have positioned Pierre Bourdieu's sociology as an indispensable work in the field of sociology right since the 1970s, as sociologists positioned themselves around it by either adhering to it or rejecting it.

The Bourdieusian School of Thought Today

As a result of growing differences, if Pierre Bourdieu set a precedent today, it is not with his former colleagues. As a result of growing differences, Jean-Claude Passeron was the first to distance himself from Pierre Bourdieu in the 1970s. He was followed by Robert Castel, Jean-Claude

Chamboredon and Claude Grignon. As for Luc Boltanski, he left the team directed by Pierre Bourdieu after having participated in the establishment of the journal *Actes de la Recherche en Sciences Sociales* in 1975. Thereafter, with Laurent Thévenot, he developed a pragmatic sociology which was critical of the Bourdieusian theory. He simultaneously denounced Pierre Bourdieu's mandarin position and his tendency to appropriate the works of his collaborators. Jeannine Verdès-Leroux strongly criticised Pierre Bourdieu in *Le Savant et la Politique. Essai sur le terrorisme sociologique de Pierre Bourdieu*[119]: she particularly criticised his refusal to acknowledge any dissent that came from his students. Most researchers who, today, adhere to the Bourdieusian theory were not present with Pierre Bourdieu in the early stages. Sociologists such as Patrick Champagne, Christophe Charle, Frédéric Lebaron, Rémi Lenoir, Gérard Mauger, Louis Pinto, Loïc Wacquant and more generally all the sociologists associated with the Centre de sociologie européenne (European Sociology Centre). In a book entitled *Pierre Bourdieu et la théorie du monde social*[120], Louis Pinto presents the Bourdieusian work as a major "symbolic revolution" that lends a fresh perspective to the understanding of the social world. The sociologists cited above, adhere to this idea and to this day, disseminate Pierre Bourdieu's concepts and analysis, especially through the journal *Actes de la Recherche en Sciences Sociales* or through works of the "Liber" collection which was founded by Pierre Bourdieu himself. Thus, the Bourdieusian school of thought still remains dynamic, despite accusations of "Bourdieuism", in other words of dogmatism, sometimes directed to researchers who adhere to it.

Although the Bourdieusian sociology still seems to be indispensable, it has nevertheless lost the central place that it occupied in the 1980s. It competes with a multitude of sociological theories: interactionism of American sociologists (Everett Hugues, Howard Becker, etc.), economies of greatness developed by Luc Boltanski and Laurent Thévenot, sociology of science and technology developed by Michel Callon and Bruno Latour.

Main Criticisms of the Bourdieusian Theory

There are many criticisms aimed at the Bourdieusian theory. The following are the four principal criticisms.

— Criticism of the Principle of Non-Consciousness

The principle of non-consciousness developed in *Le Métier de sociologue*[121], is particularly criticised. It posits that individuals are not conscious of the mechanisms used to exercise domination and that it is up to the sociologists to expose such mechanisms. This stance was somewhat detailed in *La Misère du monde.*[122] However, certain sociologists denounced it by arguing that social movements are a proof of at least a partial awareness of the mechanisms of domination among individuals who experience it.

- Criticism of Determinism

The Bourdieusian sociology is also accused of determinism. By way of their habitus, the actors, reduced to agents, are considered by Pierre Bourdieu to be simple props of the social structure. Every individual action is thus perceived to be mechanical since it is socially determined. Nevertheless, Pierre Bourdieu reiterates on several occasions that the habitus is not only a product of social structures but also a source of invention. He opposes the charges of determinism with assertions of his belief in a certain individual freedom.

- Criticism of the Inability of the Theory to Account for, as it Claims, the Entire Social World

By nature, Pierre Bourdieu's sociology comes across as a general theory which excludes any other possible reading of the functioning of society. Its hegemonic nature was thus criticised, especially by sociologists who offered complementary or alternative visions of the social world. According to these sociologists, the Bourdieusian theory would not allow to take account of all social behaviours. Some consider, in particular, that the awareness of sociological variables other than the social class, such as age or gender, offers new perspectives to understanding.

- Criticism of the Absence of Consideration of Social Change

  Pierre Bourdieu's theory is finally criticised for its inability to consider social change. By insisting on the mechanisms of reproduction of social hierarchies, the Bourdieusian explanatory system comes across as a fixist system which has trouble in taking into account historical evolutions such as the emancipation of women in the twentieth century or the actual increase in social inequalities. Pierre Bourdieu is accused of offering an inadequate idea of history, reduced to a succession of periods whose internal functioning is analysed but not the mechanisms of transition. The inability to take social change into account is denounced as a form of sociological fatalism. Pierre Bourdieu responds to this criticism by maintaining that his theory aims to bring to light the social reality in order to better report and transform it. Thus he justifies the link between his sociological work and his political engagement towards the end of his life.

The Impact of Bourdieu's Work Abroad

Pierre Bourdieu's key work, *La Distinction*[123], was translated into English in 1984. This translation enabled the circulation of the Bourdieusian thought in the United States. Pierre Bourdieu is particularly read by American researchers associated with *Cultural Studies*, a school of thought which witnessed a considerable growth during that time. His success in the United States allowed him to acquire an international audience. In the 1990s, he attended multiple conferences abroad (Germany, United States, Japan, etc.) and his works were translated into several languages. Edited in nine different languages, the works featuring in the collection "Liber" edited by Pierre Bourdieu, primarily focused on circulating path-breaking work in social sciences abroad. Thus, towards the end of his career, Pierre Bourdieu endeavoured to create an international network of researchers working towards the dissemination of ideas.

The circulation of Pierre Bourdieu's work abroad is however hindered by the distinctive syntax of his writings which is translated with a lot of difficulty and due to the France-centred nature of his theory. Besides his writing style, there are certain other aspects of the Bourdieusian work which are poorly understood across the Atlantic. In *La Noblesse d'État*,[124] for example, the sociologist focuses on institutions of higher education in France or the grandes écoles françaises, which constitute a system characteristic of the centralisation of the state in France. However, this system is a difficult concept for foreign readers who are not familiar with the French model of the state. In a broader sense, the interpretations of Pierre Bourdieu's works abroad are strongly marked by the weight of national contexts. Depending on the country reading his works, Pierre Bourdieu emerges, first and foremost, as a sociologist of education, a cultural sociologist, a French intellectual and a committed sociologist.

NOTES

119. Verdès-Leroux, J., *Le Savant et la Politique. Essai sur le terrorisme sociologique de Pierre Bourdieu* (1998), Paris, Grasset.
120. Pinto, L., *Pierre Bourdieu et la théorie du monde social* (1999), Paris, Albin Michel.

121. Bourdieu, P., Chamboredon, J.-C., Passeron, J.-C., *Le Métier de sociologue : préalables épis- témologiques* (1968), Paris, Mouton.
122. Bourdieu, P. (dir.), *La Misère du monde* (1993), Paris, Le Seuil.
123. *La Distinction. Critique sociale du jugement* (1979), Paris, Minuit.
124. *La Noblesse d'État. Grandes écoles et esprit de corps* (1989), Paris, Minuit.

Bibliographic References

- "L'illusion biographique", *Raisons pratiques. Sur la théorie de l'action* (1994), pp. 81-89 (original publication: "L'illusion biographique", *Actes de la Recherche en Sciences Sociales* (1986), Nos. 62-63, pp. 69-72).
  This very short text became a reference point with respect to sociological survey methods. In this text, Pierre Bourdieu explains the assumptions that exist at the foundation of the biographical interview carried out by numerous sociologists. He particularly emphasises the fact that the interviewee reconstructs the meaning of his existence during the course of the interview and gives a coherence to his trajectory in retrospect.
- "Espace social et pouvoir symbolique", *Choses dites* (1987), pp. 147-166.
  In this text, Pierre Bourdieu explains his theoretical positioning, which he describes as "constructivist structuralist". He shows how this theoretical choice allows him to go beyond the opposition that exists between objectivism and subjectivism, by highlighting, in particular, the aspects that differentiate his concept of social classes from the objectivist conception of social classes developed by Karl Marx.
- "Stratégies de reproduction et mode de domination", *Actes de la Recherche en Sciences Sociales* (1994), Vol. 105, pp. 3-12.
  If the reproduction of social hierarchies are prevalent in all societies, the school was not necessarily the principal instrument of this reproduction as it is the case in contemporary societies. In this article, Pierre Bourdieu shows that in pre-

capitalist societies matrimonial strategies took precedence over educational strategies and there existed family models of reproduction. He also analyses the transformation of strategies of reproduction through the emergence of the state which gave educational institutions a greater role to play in contemporary societies.

- "La terre et les stratégies matrimoniales", *Le Sens pratique* (1980), pp. 249-270 (original publication: "Les stratégies matrimoniales dans le système de reproduction", *Annales. Histoire, Sciences Sociales* (1972), Nos. 4-5, p. 1105- 1127).
  This chapter offers an analysis of family relationships within the Bearnese society which, along with the Kabylian society, forms one of the first ethnographic sites studied by Pierre Bourdieu. Matrimonial strategies carried out depending on the position occupied among the siblings were particularly studied. Thus elder and younger siblings did not have the same marriage prospects.
- "Comment peut-on être sportif?", *Questions de sociologie* (1984), pp. 173-195.
  This text by Pierre Bourdieu is an application of the Bourdieusian theory of fields in the world of sports. After having analysed the emergence of the "field of sport", Pierre Bourdieu studies the organisation of this field. A sport is considered to be a cultural practice that varies according to the social class. The strategies of distinction and more importantly, the differentiated relationship with the body produced by the habitus explain that all the classes or fractions of classes do not practise the same sports.
- "Le couturier et sa griffe: contribution à une théorie de la magie" (with Yvette Delsaut), *Actes de la Recherche en Sciences Sociales* (1975), Vol. 1, No. 1, pp. 7-36.
  This article can be read as a model for the analysis of fields. Pierre Bourdieu and Yvette Delsaut explain the genesis and functioning of the field of the French haute-couture from the 1920s to the 1970s. An emphasis is placed on the mechanisms of creation, acquisition, preservation and transmission of the symbolic value of the designer's label.
- "Espace social et espace symbolique", *Raisons Pratiques. Sur la*

théorie de l'action (1994), pp. 13-29.
In this text, Pierre Bourdieu presents, in the form of a summary, his theory of social space as a relational space. The theory is illustrated in a diagram "Space of social positions and space of lifestyles" which represent the distribution of professions, cultural activities and political stances taken based on the two axes: that of the overall volume of capital and the distribution of capital between cultural capital and economic capital. Furthermore, in this text, Pierre Bourdieu gives a clear overview of the concepts of habitus and social class.

- "L'économie des biens symboliques", *Raisons Pratiques. Sur la théorie de l'action* (1994), pp. 173-211.
This text deals with the universe of "things without a price-tag": universe of the gift, of the family, of art, of religion. In such realms, the economic value of things is euphemised or "denied" and, conversely, disinterest is valued. In order to succeed in these worlds, individuals are paradoxically better off behaving in a selfless manner.